BOOKS BY HOWARD NORMAN

The Northern Lights
The Chauffeur
The Bird Artist
The Museum Guard
The Haunting of L.
My Famous Evening
In Fond Remembrance of Me
Devotion
What Is Left the Daughter
I Hate to Leave This Beautiful Place
Next Life Might Be Kinder

I HATE TO LEAVE THIS
BEAUTIFUL PLACE

Howard Norman

Mariner Books
Houghton Mifflin Harcourt
BOSTON   NEW YORK

First Mariner Books edition 2014

For information about permission to reproduce selections from this book,
write to Permissions, Houghton Mifflin Harcourt Publishing Company,
215 Park Avenue South, New York, New York 10003.

www.hmhco.com

Library of Congress Cataloging-in-Publication Data
Norman, Howard A.
[Essays. Selections]
I hate to leave this beautiful place / Howard Norman.
pages cm
ISBN 978-0-547-38542-6   ISBN 978-0-544-31716-1 (pbk.)
1. Title.
PR9199.3.N564Z46
2013
813'.54 — dc23
[B] 2012042186

Book design by Melissa Lotfy

Printed in the United States of America
DOC 10 9 8 7 6 5 4 3 2 1

"Advice of the Fatherly Sort" first appeared, in different form, as "Birds
at Night" in *Dream Me Home Safely: Writers on Growing Up in America*
(Houghton Mifflin Company, 2003).

The poem "My Aunt Held a Grudge" by Lucille Amorak and the tale
"The Visitor Put in a Snow Globe" by Jenny Arnateeyk were translated
by the author.

Portions of "The Healing Powers of the Western Oystercatcher" appeared
previously in *Salmagundi*.

FOR DAVID ST. JOHN

CONTENTS

ACKNOWLEDGMENTS

For their deep and abiding friendship, Melanie Jackson and Alexandra Altman. And David Wyatt, for all the conversations.

INTRODUCTION

Saigyo, a poet and monk who lived in twelfth-century Japan, wrote, "A soul that is not confused is not a soul." That philosophy served me as a talisman throughout the writing of this book. I kept asking, How does someone with a confused soul, as I consider mine to be, try to gain some clarity and keep some emotional balance and find some joy, especially after a number of incidents of arresting strangeness have happened in a life?

I have always felt a bittersweet foretaste of regret when getting ready to leave certain landscapes. The title of this book comes from an Inuit folktale, one you will encounter in these pages, about a man who has been transformed into a goose. As winter fast approaches, he begins to cry out, "I hate to leave this beautiful place!"

What is remembered here? A bookmobile and an elusive father in the Midwest. A landscape painter whose plane crashed in Saskatchewan. A murder-suicide in my family's house. A Quagmiriut Inuit rock band specializing in the songs of John Lennon. And in Vermont, a missing cat, a well drilling, and my older brother's requests to be smuggled into Canada. If there is one thing that connects these disparate experiences, it is the hopeful idea of locating myself in beloved landscapes—Northern California, Nova Scotia, Vermont, the Arctic—and of describing how they offered a home for honest introspection, a place to think things through. Often I just wanted to look at birds for days on end, shore birds in particular.

Still, I would be loath to suggest that life intrinsically has themes, because it does not. In this book I narrate a life in overlapping panels of memory and experience. When Henry James used the phrase "the visitable past," he was largely referring to sites that had personal meaning for him: graveyards, archeological ruins, centuries-old cathedrals. Conversely, this present book contains memories of places that kept refusing not to visit me—unceremonious hauntings, I suppose, which were in equal measure gifts and curses. Since we are seldom stenographers of our hours and days as life unfolds, we remember events with different emotions than those we had when we originally experienced the events (as the haiku master Matsuo Basho put it), and in associative patterns rather than original chronologies. I started this book in the Villa of Fallen Persimmons in Kyoto, Japan, in a landscape I had previously only read about and seen in paintings and films. But most of it was written in Point Reyes, California, and Vermont, each a beautiful place I always hate to leave.

I HATE TO LEAVE THIS
BEAUTIFUL PLACE

ADVICE OF THE FATHERLY SORT

~~~

O N SUMMER EVENINGS IN 1964, I used to sit on the basement stairs to read and cool down. This was in Grand Rapids, Michigan. August was particularly steamy, and about seven o'clock on a Friday late in the month, I sat there and watched my older brother's girlfriend, Paris Keller ("I was named after the capital of France," she said), who was wearing blue jeans, a T-shirt, and sandals, cross her arms, raise off her shirt, and toss it into the clothes dryer. Lavender in color, it had been soaked transparent by rain on her walk to our house. Paris owned a car but liked to take long walks, too. The T-shirt read EXIST TO KISS YOU, a declaration that was both existential and, for me at age fifteen, almost cruelly erotic.

She stood there naked from the waist up. The shirt tumbled alone behind the dryer's glass window. Paris looked over at me a few times. We talked awhile. I was all but praying that the shirt needed a second cycle. Paris told me her father had been killed in the Korean War. It was the first conversation I ever wrote down. Typed it hunt-and-peck on an Olivetti manual typewriter. I made a copy on carbon paper, too. I'm looking at the pages now.

Remember carbon paper? If you handled a sheet carelessly, you would leave fingerprints on everything you touched, as if you'd broken into your own life.

I liked Paris a lot. More about her later.

To this day, my father's secret life draws certain difficult associations with an apothecary. In the Midwest in the early 1960s, the word *apothecary* had not exclusively been replaced by the term *drugstore*, or even *pharmacy*. In Dykstra's Apothecary on Division Street, the proprietor, Peter Dykstra, not only was the pharmacist but occasionally doubled as the soda jerk. In the summer months he'd hire a teenager to work the counter, which had three spin-around red leather seats, each elevated on a silver column, with a silver plate at the base, riveted to the floor. DYKSTRA'S APOTH-ECARY was stenciled in an arc of bold lettering across the wide front window. One day the radio said the summer was "proving downright tropical." The fighting in Indochina had completed its transition to the Vietnam War. You could order a root beer float, a coffee, a milk shake, a Coca-Cola—that was it. No, you could also get a grilled cheese sandwich. The apothecary carried an Afrikaans-language weekly. Mr. Dykstra had been born and raised in Johannesburg.

For concocting root beer floats, there was a helmet-headed spigot out of which a pressurized elixir hissed and gurgled into glasses the size of a small flower vase. That summer's employee was Marcelline Vanderhook, who wore a triangular paper hat bobby-pinned atop her pale blond hair. Her boyfriend, Robert Boxer, a "part-Negro boy from Ottawa Hills High School," as Marcelline said, had his driver's license and provided home deliveries using Mr. Dykstra's Studebaker. Robert was an All-State guard in basketball. Years later, he became a Rhodes scholar in art history at Oxford. Later yet, he became a successful painter in Paris and then San Francisco, specializing in portraits. I own a small oil painting of his; it shows two elderly black women sitting in wheelchairs, chatting as if on someone's porch, except the chairs are set out on a dock at Fisherman's Wharf in San Francisco. Trawlers are moored in the background.

Robert Boxer frequented the bookmobile where I was employed. The driver, a trained librarian named Pinnie Oler, would say, "Hello, Robert. I've got a Nehi orange in my ice chest here for you. You want to look at the art books, of course." Robert would sit in the bookmobile for the duration of the Dykstra's Apothecary stop, studying with great concentration books about Picasso, Matisse, Georgia O'Keeffe, and a few other world-famous artists. The art section never had more than twenty books in all.

One thing Pinnie Oler told me was that Peter Dykstra had been ostracized and "all but run out of the Dutch Reformed Church" for allowing a mixed-race couple in his employ. At the time, that was all I ever heard about this subject. Except when Robert Boxer said, "I love kicking the shit out of East Christian in basketball. They look up at the scoreboard, last two minutes, and those Hollanders get crazy bug-eyed terrified looks on their faces, all panicky like they just ate a bunch of poisonous tulips, you know? They and us worship a different Jesus, as my Alabama grandma liked to say." One other thing: Robert Boxer was Peter Dykstra's son (Robert's mother had passed away), but Robert preferred to use his mother's family name, Boxer. The emotions of it all registered in me then in an unlettered way, deep in the nerves. Any real understanding of how the apartheid system in far-flung South Africa was an intensifying element in the racist atmosphere of Grand Rapids came only in retrospect—when, in 1977, I was living in Ann Arbor and read that Robert Boxer's older brother, Reginald, had been beaten senseless during a violent protest in Detroit against the murder of the activist Steve Biko by the South African police. The name of Robert's younger brother, James, is on the Vietnam Veterans Memorial in Washington, D.C.

Through the bookmobile window, I saw my father eleven times that summer. The number has no other meaning except that it wasn't more or less. Yet I remember it was eleven. Each time he'd be sitting at the counter in Dykstra's Apothecary, chatting with Mr. Dykstra or Marcelline or Robert Boxer, drinking coffee. For the most part I'd see his handsome face in profile. He would have been thirty-eight years old. Hard to imagine that now: he's been dead for twenty years as I write this (he succumbed to lung cancer). My mother and he had met in the Belfaire Jewish Orphan Home in Cleveland, in 1933, when both were seven, and had gotten married at nineteen.

I kept these sightings to myself. Why? My mother had told me that my father was living in California. Did she know he was still in Grand Rapids? Was her statement a necessary displacement of the truth? Or did she actually believe my father was in California? My mother, Estella, died in 2009 at the age of eighty-four, and I never asked her about this. I didn't ask her a lot of things I should have.

So when the bookmobile made its scheduled forty-five-minute stop across from Dykstra's, I'd see my father with his neatly pressed trousers, white shirt buttoned to the neck, plaid sports coat, and slim build; his beautiful smile, curly short-cut brown hair, and deep blue eyes were reflected in the counter-wide mirror. Dykstra's had air conditioning. I suppose that's why my father wore his sports coat and Marcelline her button-down cotton sweater indoors. In my house, at 1727 Giddings Street, our "air conditioning" had to be set up on a day-to-day basis. It took some doing. You'd remove the ice tray from the Kelvinator's freezer, gouge out cubes with an ice pick, put the cubes in two bowls, and place one bowl in front of a small electric fan on the kitchen counter, the other in front of an identical fan on the windowsill on the opposite side of the kitchen. The kitchen table, then, was the place to sit. WGRD radio said it was on average the hottest summer of the century so far.

This is how I got the bookmobile job. One day in mid-June, about a week after Ottawa Hills High School let out, Pinnie Oler said to me, "You're every single day on this bookmobile for hours. The city's just told me I'm able to hire an assistant. Why not take the job? You know the place inside out. I'll lie about your legal age by a year. Nobody gives a shit anyway. I'll take that on myself, okay?" The job paid fifty-five cents an hour, and the hours were nine a.m. to four p.m., Tuesday through Saturday, with an hour lunch break, which I always began at noon. I'd pack a peanut butter and jelly sandwich, and Pinnie Oler would provide a bottle of Nehi orange. It was called pop, not soda. I wasn't allowed to eat my lunch inside the bookmobile, so I tried to find a shade tree to sit under. There were plenty of oaks and maples that served this need. I once woke up under a maple where I'd been napping open-mouthed, half choking on a hard-stemmed whirligig seed fallen from a low branch.

The bookmobile was an old school bus painted blue. Inside,

it had been fitted with bookshelves and two leather-topped benches. The benches had been repaired with strips of masking tape. There was a fan screwed to the dashboard and another nailed to the back shelves that covered the former emergency door. Two fans in my house, two in the bookmobile.

Pinnie Oler was, to my best guess, in his late thirties. He had a slight Dutch accent. He was about five feet nine inches tall with a thin face—a sad face, I thought. He had sandy brown hair combed straight back; you could see the comb tracks. He always wore khaki shorts, white socks, lace-up boots, and a khaki short-sleeved shirt. "My safari outfit," he called it.

My first official day on the job, he showed me how to spray the books with a special solution that killed dust mites, and how to write overdue notices and perform other clerical tasks. From the get-go I approached this employment with the utmost seriousness. I thought of studying library science. I saw myself in that world. I even entertained the possibility that Pinnie Oler's position might someday be mine. I had no earthly notion that one day bookmobiles would be extinct. I had always seen them on the streets.

Let's say you were standing next to the steering wheel and looking toward the back of the bookmobile. Filling the top three shelves on the right side was the Science category: books about zoology, astronomy, geology, medicine. There were three or four books about the Canadian Arctic. The bottom two shelves below Science were reserved for Government/Social Science. This section had a lot of books about Abraham Lincoln. Along the left side were shelves containing Fiction and Poetry (Emily Dickinson, Robert Frost, John Keats, Langston Hughes), and directly below was the shelf of Children's Books. Art was on a shelf across the back. The five slide-out wooden drawers of the card catalogue were in the back left-hand corner. On top of the drawers was a slotted box: Book Requests. At the end of my workday I'd deliver the requests to Pinnie Oler, who would submit them to the central branch library. One time I found a condom in the request box, another time a pornographic postcard bent in half, another time a handwritten note: *You will be killed for letting kikes and niggers touch our books.* I didn't show these to my boss. More typically, at day's end there would simply be four or five requests for this or that title.

My mother worked in what is now known as child care. She supervised at least a dozen young children every day at the Orthodox synagogue downtown. This meant my two younger brothers had to be at "summer camp" all day. We couldn't afford to pay the yearly dues at the synagogue, and no special dispensation was offered even though my mother worked there. Instead we belonged to what she referred to as the more "welcoming" Temple Emanuel, a Reform synagogue that provided her a more familiar if not nostalgic theology, insofar as the Belfaire Jewish Orphan Home had not followed strictly Orthodox practices.

All through my elementary and high school years, holiday events and myriad other occasions at Temple Emanuel comprised my mother's entire social life. We never had anyone over for dinner, except once in a blue moon my aunt Shirley, my mother's sister. Shirley, an officer of the temple's Sisterhood, often sat at the rabbi's table at Passover, and lorded this over my mother. ("Estella likes to fraternize with the *shvartzehs,*" meaning the black kitchen help—which was true.) Shirley had always struck me as a snob and a nag. I never did figure out where her impressive talent for condescension came from; after all, she was raised in the Belfaire Jewish Orphan Home, too. One of my aunt's primary complaints was that my mother never had anyone else over for dinner. It is possible she might've worried that my mother was isolated. More plausibly, my aunt was embarrassed by my mother's frumpy housedresses, her menial job, her introverted nature, and her absent husband—"for all intents and purposes my sister's a widow"—and she rarely invited my mother to dinner at her house, either. There it was. But by week's end my mother was simply exhausted. And she said, "I like weekends to myself."

Twice that summer my older brother, Michael, stole a car. Oddly, after each theft he waited out the police in an empty pew of Temple Emanuel or at the library table playing cards with the temple's janitor and groundskeeper. Both times, Rabbi Esrig asked what he was doing there in the middle of the day, and apparently my brother gave him an honest answer, along the lines of, "I stole a car and drove it here. It's in the parking lot." The first time, when the car—a 1958 Edsel, for God's sake, a hideously designed vehicle—was returned to its rightful owner on Union Street, the victim agreed not to press charges if my brother painted his one-story house, which my brother did, though it took him about two months. The second time, Paris dipped into her "inheritance" to bail my brother out of jail. That second victim pressed charges.

In the end Michael served six months probation, during which he was assigned the task of painting the center lines on highways with a "cleanup crew" of other parolees. The thing was, in both instances Michael had only needed transportation to the temple. Once he'd arrived there he seemed to have no further use for the stolen car. I'm not suggesting there was anything rational in any of this. Paris would've loaned him her car at the drop of a hat. She had a two-year-old black Pontiac four-door. She'd made all her payments. That was a situation heretofore unknown to me. In my house, it felt as if my mother was going to be making car payments for a hundred years.

Anyway, in late June Pinnie Oler said to me, "You always look fairly glum when you get to work. I figure you've got a lot going on at home. I'm not going to ask. Just consider this library your daytime address. But I can't let you sleep in here. I get the feeling you're about to ask to. But go ahead and consider this old bus like a café in Paris—nobody's gonna kick you out. I've never been to Paris, but I heard that's true."

Engine-wise, the bookmobile had a lot of problems: stalled out at a corner, blue hood raised, radiator geysering steam, grind of metal and friction smell, fan belt broken, oil spilling out, things like that. "Just bus problems," Pinnie Oler would call them, shrugging philosophically. Looking back, the word that I think accurately describes him is *poised*. He'd walk right up to a house, knock on the door, and when someone appeared, he'd point to the bookmobile and ask to use the telephone, and far more often than not it worked out. He would call his wife, Martha, who was a bus mechanic for the Grand Rapids school system. It must've been rare to have a woman mechanic back then. Maybe it still is. Martha would come to the rescue. She drove a green pickup truck with built-in toolboxes.

To my mind, Martha Oler was an absolutely beautiful woman. I thought she looked savvy and confident. During my months as a bookmobile assistant, she had to be called out on at least half a dozen occasions. Each time, she'd climb down from the cab of her truck, walk over to her husband, lean him against the broken-down bookmobile, and in her smudged mechanic's smock kiss him as deeply and passionately as people kissing in any movie I'd seen up to that point—right out in the open, daylight audience or no. I saw a lot through the bookmobile window. Then she'd return to the truck, get her tools, and attend to the bus problem. She was slightly taller than Pinnie, had dark red hair and a quick, lip-biting smile, and always leaned inside the bookmobile to say, "Hey, sport, fancy seeing you here!" That was her little joke, me being a fixture like I was.

The bookmobile made eight official stops per day. Hillcrest Elementary, the public swimming pool, Mills Retirement Village, Blodgett Memorial Hospital, across from Dykstra's Apothecary, Mulick Park Elementary School, Union High School, and the YMCA. But in the summer of 1964, Pinnie Oler also made, a minimum of twice a week, what he called an unscheduled stop. This was in front of his own house, at 58 Wycliffe Drive NE. The first time he made this unscheduled stop, he switched off the ignition and said, "There's a park nearby. Take a Nehi orange or keep filling out overdue notices, whatever you want. Me and Martha are trying to make a baby." He turned the roundabout handle to open the door, stepped out onto the street, went to the front of the bookmobile, and propped open the hood so it looked like the bus had broken down. "For appearance' sake," he said. His wasn't a front door he had to knock on. Two Nehi orange sodas later—add to that sitting in the park reading a book about adventures in the far north of Canada, dangling my feet in a pond that was home to two aggressive swans to watch out for, and nodding off under an oak for a quick nap on a sultry afternoon—I went back to the bookmobile. There I found Pinnie Oler sitting in the driver's seat, the motor idling. Martha was browsing the

Science section. "Martha's got the afternoon off," he said. "She's going to get some reading in."

It was about this time that I started to write letters to other people's fathers. I wrote a lot of these letters in the bookmobile during lulls. I wrote them on the backs of overdue notices, upward of ten notices per letter.

First I made a list of fathers. All told, there were twenty-two. I wrote to Jerry Boscher's father, Marcia Eldersveld's, Paul Bigelow's, Shawnay Smith's, Gary van Eerden's, Becky Marcellus's, Jay Osherow's, Stephen Peck's, Tommy Sturdevant's, Esme Carlyle's father (he was an elementary school principal), Ellen Hake's, Brian Siplon's, Sara Schoen's, Genevieve T. Park's, Eric Klein's, Eileen Heuvelhorst's, Darlene Diane Johnson's, Bobby Fodor's, Mandez Iver Garnes's, Yvonne Muller's, Nancy Wong's, and Ira and Jay Dembinksky's father.

I never sent a single letter; in that sense, my epistolary life was willfully unrequited. But I didn't throw them away, either. Plus, I made carbon copies. "A letter never sent is a kind of purgatory," writes Chekhov. What made me write all those letters? The basic desire to speak to *any* father with a sense of intimacy, I suppose. Being able to organize emotions, the direct address, the implorations and requests, the letting off of steam, the indictments, the complaints, the attempt to feel things deeply. And since I was composing these letters on pieces of paper with the words *Overdue Notice* at the top, they must've been written with an abiding sense of urgency, not to mention some notion of imposing a penalty. No single example can fully represent this veritable fugue state of letter writing. But here's one written to Mandez Garnes's father, whose first name was Jacob.

Dear Mr. Garnes,

You probably remember that I'm friends with your son Mandez and that I've been at your house. You probably remember that at your barbeque Mandez and I took our chicken and potato salad over by the guest house. Mandez told me the guest house was going to become his own private room. It was going to be his birthday present when he turned sixteen. I work in the bookmobile and have some time to think about important things. One of these things is that last week you might remember seeing me in front of the Majestic Theatre. I wasn't short on money for a ticket. I didn't need to ask you for money because I work in the bookmobile, as I said. I don't remember a lot of things my own father said but he called that kind of movie a shoot 'em up. Why I'm writing this letter is for the following reason. I want to tell you that I thought it was wrong of you to embarrass Mandez when he found out he was short of ticket money himself. You said it builds character to earn your own money and why should you pay for Mandez, he's already fifteen. My own father embarrasses me every day by not being around. Mandez is lucky you're around but you didn't have any cause to embarrass Mandez that way, I think. You could just as easily of given him the ticket money and talked to him father son in private later on. That's all of it. By the way something you should know is that Mandez is good at earning money. For instance there's nobody better than your son at finding money people dropped under the bleachers at Ottawa Hills stadium, during football games. Maybe you didn't know that every Saturday and Sunday morning Mandez walks around under the bleachers and finds money like that. Were you ever that smart when you were 15? Maybe you should give that some thought. I don't think

Mandez enjoyed the movie very much because of all of what you did.

With sincerity,

I stopped writing these letters when school started again, but by then my archive contained two hundred, give or take. I'd purchased two manila envelopes, placed the originals in one, the carbons in another. I stuffed both in the bottom drawer of a metal cabinet in the basement of our house, a drawer otherwise crammed with Belfaire Jewish Orphan Home newsletters from the 1930s.

On July 5 — I remember the date because I watched Peter Dykstra take down from the apothecary window an American flag he'd displayed on Independence Day — Robert Boxer brought his grandmother to the bookmobile. She had just been in the apothecary with my father, her grandson Robert, and her son-in-law Peter Dykstra. I saw my father step outside, walk down the street, and stand by the bus stop about a block away. Mrs. Boxer was quite large, about sixty-five years of age, I'd guess, and confined to a wheelchair, so Robert had to carry her up the three steps. He was strong, but it definitely took some effort. At the landing, she said, "Now, see, Robert, aren't you glad I don't eat those Snickers bars like I used to?" Robert started laughing so hard he almost dropped his grandmother, but he kept his balance, navigated to a bench, and set his grandmother down on it. He sat next to her, catching his breath. "My grandmother's doing deliveries with me today," Robert said to me and Pinnie Oler.

"I'm keeping on my church hat," she said. "It's good for these hot sunny days and I am easily flushed. And if my blood heats up too much, well, my grandson Robert can tell you, I have been known to faint."

"You're strong as a horse, Grandma," Robert said. "I don't know why you present yourself this way all the time. I've never seen you faint."

"Heat stroke, it's called," Mrs. Boxer said. "And the only reason, Robert, you have not seen me faint from it is because you never happen to be there."

"My loving pharmacist father says you're generally in very good health," Robert said.

"My own mother lived to be one hundred and two," she said.

"I've heard that rumor," Robert said. "I've heard that rumor a thousand times."

Naturally, Pinnie offered Mrs. Boxer a Nehi orange, which she accepted. Mrs. Boxer, Pinnie, Robert, and I were all drinking Nehi orange. "This bookmobile's a regular speakeasy," she said, but I didn't know what a speakeasy was. Once she got settled with her drink, Mrs. Boxer started in on "the man who's always at the counter." I quickly realized she was referring to my father, though she didn't know the man was my father; nobody knew he was my father except for me. "Every time our church's station wagon delivers me to visit Robert at work, that man's there. Well, maybe not *every* time, but almost. Yes, sir, just about every time. I don't know, there's something *uncomfortable* about him. O vale of sorrows, O Lord in heaven, forgive me for speaking with suspiciousness toward a man living or dead, but *this* man—he's a snake charmer. Yes, sir, he could charm a snake."

I was feeling humiliated at this point. I started to page through a book of photographs of polar bears and Eskimos and stark landscapes.

"That's not how you raised me to talk," Robert said. "You're becoming what you say you didn't like about your own mother in Alabama, Grandma. An old back-porch gossip. Larry's never been anything but friendly to me. He's got a name, by the way. Larry."

Pinnie adjusted the dashboard fan so Mrs. Boxer could benefit more from it.

"Larry might be unemployed," Pinnie said. "Just because he dresses like a toothbrush salesman doesn't mean he's employed selling toothbrushes." Truth was, I had no idea what my father did for a living. Maybe he did sell toothbrushes.

"That's also true," Mrs. Boxer said. "It's my son-in-law I'm worried about, though. Peter's a good man, but he shouldn't agree with all this man's opinions — is *my* opinion."

"He's got opinions. He's got opinions. And some are excitable. But Larry speaks like a very well-educated man, Grandma," Robert said. "Okay, he's maybe *uncomfortable*, like you say. However you mean that."

"I've never once heard him say anything personal about his life," Mrs. Boxer said. "Such as, does he have a wife, does he have a family? Nothing."

"Well," Pinnie said, "if he doesn't have a wife and family, he's not going to mention them, is he?"

There was agreement on this sentiment all around. Everyone drank their Nehi oranges in silence. Then Mrs. Boxer looked at me and said, "Did you ever meet this Larry? Come to think of it, Howard, I've never seen you inside the apothecary, come to think of it. You're either in this bookmobile or you're standing next to this bookmobile."

"I've seen him through the window," I said.

"Not quite the same thing as being in a room with somebody, Lord knows," Mrs. Boxer said.

"Maybe he's got no other daytime place to go," Pinnie said. "It's a free country, as long as he pays for his coffee."

The conversation moved on.

During a mid-July stop in front of Union High School, a man returned a book on interlibrary loan, *North American Indian Waterfowl Traps, Weirs, and Snares*. At such moments, the basic transaction of borrowing or returning, I would often attempt to be a student of people. I'd scrutinize a face, size up a person, make a private assessment, indulge in speculation as to what sort would be interested in this or that particular book. I'd even speculate about which room a person read in at home—kitchen, living room, bedroom, screened-in porch—and other sorts of domestic tableaux, attempting to think narratively, to put each person at the center of the story of his or her life.

One day Pinnie caught me exhibiting a severe frown, part of an overall expression of doubt toward a borrower, a woman who was teaching a summer course at Union High. Soon after this teacher left the bookmobile, he said, "That look you get on your face, it isn't exactly welcoming. It doesn't fit the etiquette of my bookmobile. You squint like you're trying to hypnotize somebody. You should see yourself. Goodness sake, the person's just returning a book. You make it like you want to sit them down in an empty room at the police station. You know, bare light bulb overhead. 'Sir—ma'am—why'd you choose that particular book, anyway?' Like every day's an episode of *Dragnet*. Try and stop doing that, okay?"

That evening, without officially noting on an interlibrary loan form that it had been punctually returned to the bookmobile, I slipped *North American Indian Waterfowl Traps, Weirs, and Snares* into my weather-beaten knapsack, in there with the tangerine peels from my lunch. I didn't want to wait for the book to go through channels before I could study it. I stopped to sit on a park bench on my way home. After a quick perusal of some of the illustrations, I was hooked. I immediately felt the excitement of trying, as soon as possible, to apply ancient, "well-traveled" techniques of capturing ducks—maybe even a swan—to my almost nightly visits to Reeds Lake in Ramona Park. Reeds Lake was my secret haunt that summer.

While I wasn't legally sanctioned to drive until I was sixteen, truth be told I drove a car nearly every night. I'd been anxious to drive. (In the bookmobile I'd read enough of *On the Road* by Jack Kerouac to grasp its hipster restlessness as a possibility for me, say, a year or two down the line. What's more, I'd secretly put Maynard G. Krebs, the stereotypical beatnik character on *The Many Loves of Dobie Gillis*, with his goatee, unkempt clothes, and laid-back cool, in the same light. Kerouac and Krebs were my earliest icons of an independent life.) In fact, I'd already purchased a beat-to-crap 1960 Ford, whose grille had been stove in by a pickup truck and never repaired. I didn't care. That car represented my future, sitting day and night in my driveway. It had cost $200. Paris Keller helped me out there. I had only mentioned my desire to own it and she loaned me $150. She even went to East Grand Rapids to take it for a test drive, telling the owner she herself was interested in buying it. I suppose that had some truth to it, since she was the one who signed the bill of sale, and, the next day, she transferred the title over to my name. I had no idea how to thank her.

As often as seven nights a week, I'd wait until my mother was asleep, the radio always on next to her bed (my mother was ever on the alert for tornado warnings; we had a tornado shelter, with a basement entry, stocked with cans of Campbell's soup and two bottles of whiskey, and some nights my mother slept down there), then I'd drive the thirty or so blocks to Reeds Lake.

I had practically memorized the driver's test manual and was careful to stay below the speed limit, hands at ten o'clock and two o'clock on the wheel, navigating the streets to the wealthy section of town. Some people had lakefront houses with wraparound porches and cabin cruisers moored in boat garages. One reason I went to the lake was to swim near the faux Mississippi paddle-wheel steamer, which, a decade earlier, had been the feature attraction of a popular amusement park, but now it was in shabby disrepair, in dry-dock on scaffolding, propped up a few feet out of the water, so on a windy day waves lapped at its hull. Most people I knew preferred to swim at public swimming pools, the more adventuresome ones in the Thornapple River.

On an exceedingly hot day during the last weeks of school the previous year, my best friend, Paul Amundson, and I played hooky, walked about three miles to the Thornapple, stripped down, and prepared to go for a swim in the shallows, mostly shrouded by enormous oak and willow trees, on a beautiful stretch of the river. When we stepped out from behind an oak, we heard laughter and playful shouting. We immediately got dressed and investigated, and to our astonishment discovered our English teacher, Kathy Woods, skinnydipping with her fiancé, whom she'd introduced to our after-school creative writing club. "Class," she'd said, "I'd like you to meet my fiancé, Mr. Williams. He's a policeman. But he's extra-special and different, because he writes for newspapers, and he's writing his own poetry, too. Don't be afraid to ask questions just because a real writer is visiting, okay?"

Behind the tree, Paul became a little panicky. "We have two

choices. We can stay and watch, or we can get out of here fast." I voted for staying. Paul said, "But what if I see something I can't forget? What'll I do then?" I could only come up with, "Just remember as much as you can for the rest of your life." Paul started to walk away. He didn't look back; I looked back, then ran and caught up with my friend. "What I think's best," Paul said, "is to give people their privacy." I thought it was the most adult, dignified thing I'd ever heard.

The following Monday, an "exercise in description" was due in Miss Woods's English class. I worked on mine for hours over the weekend, typing version after version on the Olivetti. On Tuesday before English class, the last period of the day, Miss Woods asked for a private conference. So I stayed after, and she said, "I want to speak with you about your three pages of description. First, let me point out that I only asked for two pages. You got a little carried away. That meant I had to read more of your writing than anyone else's. But okay. All right. That's not a crime, is it?

"The assignment was to provide a description of anything you wanted and to give what you write a lot of thought. And I think your writing is excellent. But I took note of a few things. Let me see here . . . Oh, yes, here on page two. Where you write how this teacher and this policeman—let me quote you—'entwined their clothes in knots before they jumped into the river.' Let's examine this sentence. You really don't need the word *entwined* to describe knots, do you? Knots are by definition entwined, aren't they? Now, I won't tell the principal you were skipping school. That would be hypocritical of me. Fine, then. Now that we have an understanding, I'll trust you to keep my truancy to yourself— and I'll do the same for you. Both of us will have to live with the fact that we skipped school on an unbearably hot day and ended up at the same swimming hole. Funny how life is. All right, you're free to go now. By the way, I haven't breathed a word about this to my fiancé. You remember he's a policeman, right?"

As for Reeds Lake in the summertime, its nocturnal waters, moonlight, starlight, and especially the trumpeter swans ghosting along the hull of the paddle-wheel steamer, seldom failed to provide a reprieve from a fifteen-year-old's operatic despairs. Also, I found it was a place where I could think things through. Not that I ever succeeded in thinking anything through to perfect clarity, or even usefulness, but I was aware of trying to. In essence I went to the lake to think. And to slip into the water and dog-paddle a few yards behind the swans, I suppose daring them to turn and unfold with startling velocity those S-curved necks and strike me with their beaks. That had happened only once, when I was caught unawares, daydreaming at night near the paddle wheeler, and a swan was right there and it was too late to swim away or dive underwater. For a week I had a bruise risen black-and-blue above my right eye. I might've been blinded by a swan, which would at least have been unique. Apart from that skirmish, I always had the rarest sense of a peaceful heart at Reeds Lake. Yet the most magical times for me were whenever enough gulls — they flew in from Lake Michigan — gathered on the paddle wheeler, so that the shifting weight of them would make the boat begin to turn, if only a foot or two at most. I always hated to leave that place. Every time, I hated to leave.

After studying *North American Indian Waterfowl Traps, Weirs, and Snares* for five or six nights in a row, I felt prepared to apply my one-book scholarship to the real thing. At a hardware store I purchased strips of balsa wood, framing wood, nails, twine, and a length of window screen for the trap's walls (my use of the wire screen was cheating a little in authenticity). Water weeds, for camouflage, I found at Reeds Lake. There I was, waist-deep in the water at about two a.m., the lake misting, completing the construction of a trap. Given my limited carpentry skills, focus and intent were not enough; the result was less trap than contraption. Still, I situated it just beneath the paddle wheeler and fixed it to a splintered part of the hull with twine. When I first entered the water, ten or so mallards scooted off, honking in alarm. I placed "duck pellets" and bread crusts on a small platform inside the trap and retreated a dozen yards, sinking until I was neck-deep in water. From there I kept the trap under surveillance, vaguely aware of a pair of swans off to my left that appeared to be sleeping, heads tucked into back feathers, all exquisiteness in their moonlight repose.

Soon the mallards cautiously drew close to me. At such proximity, they were, in the intricacies of their plumage, surprisingly lovely. The expressiveness of their muttering, gargling, and quick nostril-fluting, the repertoire of coded signals, was hypnotic. I suppose I was lost in all of that when, quite suddenly, a swan reared back, water fantailing in moonlit droplets from its wings spread full width, then lurched forward, emitting a kind of choking hiss, hell-bent on destruction. In its approach the swan sent the mallards packing, then darted out its head directly into the trap, lifted it up, and finally wore it like a fencer's protective mask. Caught like that, the swan went berserk, violently shaking its head and neck back and forth, attempting to disengage itself from the trap.

However much I was taking this all in, I hardly expected the swan to have the sheer strength to push the trap underwater in the direction of the paddle wheeler, and in a few moments I grew terrified because it hadn't surfaced again. I didn't know whether to wait it out or swim over and in some sort of adrenaline rush attempt to intervene — how would a person even do that with a swan? I should not have thought but acted, because all motion had stopped: the swan was now visibly floating, but drowned.

Back to the evening when I sat on the basement stairs talking to Paris Keller. I told her about the letters I was writing. I don't know why I did that. Perhaps her sheer presence, the bold, natural way she had exposed her breasts, turned the laundry room into a confessional. Perhaps I wanted her to think I was interesting in some way, that I had depths. "You put them in envelopes and put stamps on them and everything?" she asked. "You paid good money at the post office and everything?"

"Yes."

"But you haven't sent a one. Not one letter."

I walked over to the metal cabinet and kicked the bottom drawer. "They're all in here, Paris," I said.

The clothes dryer had stopped spinning and Paris took out the T-shirt and, facing away from me, slipped it back on. "It's my fault I was standing here looking like I looked," she said. "But once you saw that, you made the decision to stay and talk. Polite to stay and talk, but not so polite to stare, my friend. You could've sat a few rungs up, huh?"

"You could've asked me for a spare shirt."

"Touché," she said. "Well, I have to get going. Your brother and I are going to the drive-in and doing stuff after."

"Goodbye, Paris," I said. "You won't tell anybody about the letters, will you?"

She made a gesture like she was zipping closed her mouth with her finger. Then she comically mumbled, "Mum's the word."

There are certain incidents that will not allow you to forget them. The Japanese have a saying: "Rain enters your diary." It refers to the melancholy that is forever part of your personal history. Later, you find the diary and read it and rediscover how you were experiencing life. The diary remembers for you.

When I assert that I can recall only one conversation with my father with any confident degree of accuracy, I mean it. That is because I wrote about it in a diary.

The conversation took place because my father, listening to WGRD in Dykstra's Apothecary, had heard the announcement that I had won $666 in a contest.

I scarcely saw my older brother that summer. "Michael lives on another planet," my mother said. "It's right here in Grand Rapids, but it's another planet." He was eighteen. Black chinos, black shit-kicker boots, duck's-ass haircut, indoor pallor. Always exhibiting a pained, wistful expression. Cut from the James Dean or Sal Mineo mold. He was working different jobs—he did grounds-keeping work at a cemetery for a few weeks, for example—and the rest of the time he spent with Paris. He had an apartment on Union Street. I always wanted to see it, but I didn't know the exact address. I thought he may have been living there with Paris. "I'd venture to guess they cohabit" is how my mother put it— her vocabulary was inventive. Truth be told, I didn't know much about my older brother's life at all.

As I said, my Ford was parked in our driveway, license plate and all. One morning in late July, at just after eight—the summer-camp bus had just picked up my two younger brothers at the corner and my mother had already left for work—I was eating cereal and drinking orange juice at the kitchen table, listening to WGRD. The disk jockey, "Mad Marty" Sobieski, whose morning rock-and-roll program ran from seven a.m. to noon, was gabbing away between tunes. His signature shout-out during his show was "Mad Marty's throwin' a party!" Sometimes he'd add, "Former president Dwight D. Eisenhower said he'd drop by, but he canceled. Oh, well, maybe next time, Ike."

That morning, Mad Marty talked a blue streak about the "license plate lottery." In fact, he was about to announce the first winner. The deal was, WGRD's director of programming, at eight-fifteen sharp, would reach into a bin containing, on strips of paper, the license plate numbers of "every legally registered car in Grand Rapids, Michigan." There was a lot of excitement at the radio station. Though WGRD was just background noise while I ate breakfast, when the winning number was announced, a bell went off in my head. I turned up the volume. Mad Marty repeated the number again and again. "If this is your license plate number, call Mad Marty right up here at WGRD, then come on down and collect the prize money of *six hundred sixty-six dollars and no cents!* You heard me—six hundred sixty-six smackeroos!"

By now you've figured out that the winning number was on my brand-new license plate. I'd memorized it because, besides my telephone number, it was the only number that meant anything to me. Still, I went out to the driveway just to make sure.

I telephoned the radio station. Then I called Pinnie Oler at home and told him my news. "I take it you'll give at least half to your mother," he said. "Okay, then, get downtown and become a millionaire. Take the day off work. I'll consider it that you called in sick. See you tomorrow morning. I'm going to have to start charging you for every Nehi orange from now on." I didn't know what to say. Pinnie interpreted my silence. "Jesus, Howard, just *kidding.* Such a serious kid. Your sense of humor's in the trash can."

I took three connecting buses downtown to WGRD. I never thought I'd ever get to meet Mad Marty Sobieski in the flesh. He was a specter, a disembodied voice like the Wizard of Oz. Turned out he was about forty years old, wore a suit and tie and owl-eyed black-rimmed glasses and bespoke shoes. And he took all of two minutes with me.

He came out of his broadcast booth and had some lackey take a snapshot of us both holding the check. "Well, kiddo, congratu- lations. Don't let all this cash give you too much of a hard-on. On second thought, you look like you could use it! Ha ha ha!" He shook my hand in exaggerated pump-handle fashion, said "Look at that scowl! Groovy. Too cool for school," and disap- peared back into his booth. I heard the beginning of "Baby Love" by the Supremes. By the time I made it to the ground floor and stood gawking at my check, the lobby's sound system was playing "Do Wah Diddy Diddy" by Manfred Mann. And when I got on the first bus and turned on my transistor radio, Mad Marty was saying, "Two in a row by Mr. Manfred Mann—oooooh, I just can't *help* myself!" And then he played "Leave My Kitten Alone."

One day in early August at about six-thirty p.m., Paris drove up and parked in front of our house. I was sitting on the porch. "Your brother's got the flu. He's throwing up and complaining. Getting the flu in summer's a real drag. Well, at least he doesn't have to paint that house for a couple days, right? Wanna go to the mov- ies?"

"I don't think so."

"Aw, come on, fuckstick." That was her pet name for me.

"I don't know. What's playing?"

"*Zorba the Greek*'s supposed to be good. It's at the Majestic."

"You want to go to the movies with *me*? I don't get it."

"Tell me the truth. Have you ever been to the movies with a girl?"

"Nope."

"See how easy telling the truth is with me?"

"I'd better ask my brother."

"He suggested it, actually."

"Still, I'd better check with him."

"Just call him up, why don't you?"

"Okay."

I went inside and dialed Michael's number, which was on a piece of paper held by a magnet on the refrigerator door. I let it ring and ring. He didn't pick up.

Back on the porch I said, "There's no answer. What's *Zorba the Greek* about, anyway?"

"A Greek person named Zorba. His adventures."

"What time's the show?"

Paris was wearing jeans and a T-shirt that read ENTER AT YOUR OWN RISK. I didn't comment, but she saw I'd taken notice. She looked at her watch. "Twenty-five minutes. We can just make it."

Against my better judgment, or on behalf of it, I don't know which, I got in the front seat. "We can each pay for our own ticket, okay?" she said. "That make you less nervous?"

"Fine."

We both bought popcorn and settled into seats in the middle section, about a fourth of the way down the aisle. The Majestic was a magnificent World War Two–era movie house with a cathedral ceiling, plush carpeting, and employees dressed like bellhops; it was all going to seed but was still the best theater in town. The air conditioning felt good. This showing was sparsely attended: the closest person was at least four rows away.

After the coming attractions, the movie got under way. When Anthony Quinn started to demonstrate his famous finger-snapping, drunken, all-joyful-abandon Zorba dance, Paris, staring at the screen, unbuckled my belt. She lowered the zipper of my blue jeans, reached in, and started to slowly (and allow me to say expertly, though I'd had nothing to compare it to) stroke me. This went on well past Zorba's dance. At one point, she leaned close and said, "It's okay, darling. It's okay, I'm in no hurry. The movie's hardly halfway through I bet." She had on some subtle, breathtaking perfume, and I think it was that, mixed with the tangy fragrance of her sweat, dried in the coolness of the theater, as much as the ministrations of her fingers which drove me to distraction. When I pulsed hard and exploded, thickly, into her hand, she whispered, lipsticked lips touching my ear, "That feels nice," speaking for both of us, I hoped. Then she got me all tucked back in and zipped up, and even buckled my belt. Whispering again, she said, "A nice girl would go to the ladies' room now, but I don't want to miss any of the movie. It's making me want to go to a Greek island."

We didn't speak about this in the car. In fact, we never spoke about it ever. About a week later, I received the first of many telephone calls like this one: "Hello, Howard? This is Jacob Garnes, Mandez's father."

There in my kitchen, between pounding heartbeats and hard-to-catch breaths, I immediately understood that Paris had mailed my letters. It had to have been Paris. No one else knew where the letters were hidden.

. . .

27

As for the conversation with my father that entered my diary: When I got back home from WGRD with my check for $666, I sat at the kitchen table looking at it. I may have had a second bowl of cereal. No more than half an hour later, Mr. Dykstra's Studebaker appeared in the driveway. I stood at the window and watched my father crouch out from the driver's seat. I couldn't imagine how he persuaded Mr. Dykstra to loan him the Studebaker—the thought occurred to me that he'd stolen it. Either way, there it was, right in the driveway.

My father hadn't noticed me yet. He was dressed in light brown slacks, brown loafers, a white short-sleeved shirt. I could see his sports coat slung over the front passenger seat. Really, he was as handsome as a movie star. He glanced briefly at the house, walked to the back of the Studebaker, popped open the trunk, took out a hammer, slammed shut the trunk, laid his left hand flat on the trunk lid, and brought the hammer straight down on his thumb. He winced and slumped in pain, then closed his eyes and leaned against the trunk for a moment, as if he were about to faint. He tossed the hammer in the back seat and walked into the house.

He hadn't been in the house for well over a year. What I theorized right away was that he'd battered his thumb in order to deflect my mother's anger and suspicion away from him. Desperate and inane—he was a coward that way. My theory wasn't farfetched at all: I'd seen him invent such distractions three or four times before. This time the bizarre plan didn't have its intended effect because my mother wasn't home. To this day, I'm amazed that he didn't even know her work schedule.

I was alone in the house, sitting at the kitchen table, the check next to my cereal bowl. My father stood in the doorway, appraising me. "You've gotten too skinny," he said. "You're a skinny goat, son."

"Since I'm your son, does that make you a goat, too?"

"That's witty. That's thinking on your feet."

"What happened to your thumb, there, Dad?"

He held out his hand and studied it, as if beholding an object separate from himself. "Oh, that," he said. "I accidentally slammed it in the car door. Get me some ice cubes and a towel, will you?"

I stayed at the table, trying to stare him down. It must've looked stupid. I was dressed in a black T-shirt and blue jeans and black high-tops, no socks. I had let my hair grow. I was the only one among my friends and acquaintances who had a ponytail.

"What's that on the back of your head?" my father asked. He was nothing if not well groomed. He always kept his hair in what he called a "businessman's cut." When I didn't answer, he said, "Cat got your tongue?"

He walked to the refrigerator, opened the door, took an ice cube tray from the freezer, set the tray on the kitchen table, and pried out some cubes with his ever-handy jackknife. The jackknife was on a key chain. He wrapped the ice cubes in a dishtowel and sat down across from me at the table. He swathed his thumb in the towel.

"Slammed the door on it, huh?" I said.

"You aren't hard of hearing. That's good. That's a good thing."

"It must hurt."

"What's that on the back of your head?"

"Where's the hammer? Still in the back seat?"

"What hammer, exactly, are you referring to?"

We stared at each other for a long, silent moment. I could hear the refrigerator humming.

"I guess it's a badge of individuality, that goddamn ponytail. It's a short ponytail. But still noticeable. Is there something you want to tell me?"

"Like what?"

"Like you might not be the type of young man interested in girls."

"I don't get what you mean."

"Never mind."

"I see you've got Mr. Dykstra's Studebaker out there."

This stymied my father—how would I know whose car it was? How had I come by such knowledge?

"It's a borrowed car, true enough."

"Borrowed from whom I already said I know."

"I'm very impressed by your diction. It's like Shakespeare."

"Too bad it doesn't have California plates. I've never seen California plates."

"The car I keep in California has California plates, naturally."

"Naturally."

"Maybe—and I just thought of this—maybe you've been low on cash and couldn't afford a decent haircut. Maybe that hairdo's the result of financial constrictions around this house in my absence. I send your mother money, you know. She's got money I send her for house expenses. Come to think of it, I could give you a haircut right now, in the kitchen here. Just with a scissors."

"No thanks."

"I've had the same haircut since I was in the air force, flying over Europe. The Italian campaign. When a haircut suits you, it suits you no matter how the world changes."

The ice cubes were melting out of the towel.

"Speaking of license plates," he said. He adjusted the towel and his face cringed.

"What about them?"

"Let's reverse the situation here, shall we?"

"What do you mean?"

"Let's reverse the situation. Say you dropped by my place of residence and said you were temporarily not flush. Do you think for one minute I'd hesitate to reach directly into my pocket, snap out my wallet, and hand you a roll of five-dollar bills, or tens, or twenties, you being my son in need? Peel off a few fifties for you? Right on the spot to help out my son?"

"I'm fifteen, Dad. I work in a bookmobile. Maybe you didn't know that. Maybe that news didn't reach you in California. I'm never flush."

"Speaking of license plates, you're pretty flush now, aren't you?"

"Were you listening to WGRD, maybe? Like Mom says, miracles never cease."

"Your mother and I don't agree on that. I think miracles cease the minute you're born."

"Mom's life is not easy. I don't know what yours is."

"Imagine how proud I felt—just dropped in to have a cup of coffee at a counter on Division Street, on comes the radio, and on comes my own son's name spoken by WGRD. If that's not good news first thing in the morning, I don't know what is."

"It was to me. I'm giving half to Mom."

"Hey, know what? I could give you a lift over to Old Kent Bank, you could cash your check, and I'd be right there with you."

"Where've you mainly been this past year?"

"Mostly California."

"Oh, sure."

"Mostly. Not always. Mostly."

"Well, I think some of that money you say you sent didn't get here. Mom's not exactly flush."

"Whoa, now, son. Hold on. Just hold on. The adult finances — no, that's not your business."

"I'll give you a hundred dollars."

"How about a three-way split. Me. You. Your mother. Just like a family. Of course, it'd be a short-term loan, mind you."

"We could stop at Blodgett Hospital. They could look at your thumb."

"No, no — life's generally an emergency, but this thumb's not."

"I don't understand."

"Let's drop it. How's your job in the bookmobile? What's your wages?"

"I'm paid six hundred sixty-six dollars an hour, Dad. Since you're all of a sudden so interested. I file cards in the card catalogue. You once told me you used to read books. You should drop by, find a book to read. When it becomes overdue, I'll send you a notice. Give me your address, just in case."

We drove in the Studebaker to Old Kent Bank. The teller had heard the WGRD lottery on the radio and commented on my luck. "You don't need to deposit it," the teller said, "because we'll hold the amount against your mother's account overnight. But it's WGRD's check. It's going to be fine. Congratulations." He counted out the cash and pushed it toward me.

In the parking lot I handed my father ten ten-dollar bills. No more bargaining. No further discussion. It felt as if I'd compensated him for his rare visit. I told him that I wanted to take a bus back, and he said, "A nice summer's day to be young with cash in your pocket." He got into the Studebaker. The windows were rolled down. "The money I gave you would buy maybe two hundred cups of coffee in Dykstra's," I said. I turned away, not wanting to see the expression on his face. I'd rather have imagined it. I heard the Studebaker drive off.

I'd gotten only a block or two away from the bank when my father pulled the car up alongside the curb about ten feet from where I was walking. He honked the horn in a snippet of Morse code. I looked over. "Men shake hands when they part company after a business arrangement," he said. I walked up to the car and we shook hands.

When my mother dragged herself in from work, she said, "I'm beat." I'd already cleaned up the kitchen. She liked a clean kitchen when she got home. I handed her a wad of cash and told her that I'd won $666 in a contest on WGRD. I told her I had just given her $566. She was flabbergasted and had to sit down. "Oh, my," she said. "I had no idea. No idea at all. Miracles never cease." She set the money down on the kitchen table and got a glass from the cabinet. She filled the glass with water and drank it. "So, you kept a hundred dollars for yourself, sweetheart. That's good. That's a lot of gas money—when you turn sixteen and start to drive, for instance. But why not splurge a little now? Why not take a friend to see *Zorba the Greek*? It's still playing at the Majestic. I hear it's wonderful. You should see it, honey."

"I'll think about it, Mom."

"All right. I'm going to have a cup of coffee, then go meet your brothers at the bus. Want to come with?"

Four days after the incident with the swan, Pinnie Oler did something unprecedented, which was to say, "How about lunch with me today?" Right away I knew something was wrong. I soon discovered that he'd put some advance thought into this because he'd brought along a checkered tablecloth. He parked the bookmobile near a small park full of big sycamore trees, carried the tablecloth and his lunch pail along with two bottles of Nehi orange over to one of the sycamores, spread out the cloth, and sat down.

I stood by the bookmobile with my lunch in a paper bag, watching, postponing what I felt was going to be a bad moment. I had no choice, however, but to go over and sit under the tree. I had taken only one bite of my peanut butter and jelly sandwich when Pinnie unfolded the *Grand Rapids Press,* flipped through it, found the page he wanted, and laid it flat on the tablecloth. I saw he had circled a small article in pencil.

"What's that?" I asked.

It is remarkable how long you can suspend a peanut butter sandwich in midair and stop time, hoping perhaps to turn back the clock, return to the life you led before, say, you stole a book. I noticed Pinnie staring at my levitated sandwich, so I set it down on the bag. "There's an interesting article in the paper today," he said. And he read the three-paragraph article about the police going out to investigate the death of a swan. Apparently two young women walking home from playing tennis had discovered the swan washed up on the shore of Reeds Lake. I recall this sentence: "Police say the swan died from the malicious handiwork of a cruel person." The investigation was ongoing, the article said; swans fell under the jurisdiction of the Parks Department, and the perpetrator would, if identified, be fined and possibly serve jail time.

"Sad about the swan," I said.

"You know who my favorite author is?" Pinnie asked.

"You never told me."

"Arthur Conan Doyle. You know, the Sherlock Holmes mysteries."

"I'd like to read one someday."

"As you know, my bookmobile's got quite a few."

"If I don't know that, who does?"

"Right. Well, I mention Sherlock Holmes because it's interesting to see how clues come together in those stories. I know they're made-up stories, of course. But that's what good fiction can do, isn't it, give you a different way of looking at real life."

"I'd need to think about that. Maybe tonight I'll think about it."

"Hey, take out any Sherlock Holmes you want. I'll personally cover it if you're delinquent in returning it on time. No problem in the least."

"That's nice of you."

"You get peanut butter and jelly every damn day, don't you? I don't think I could do that. I have to vary lunch a little. Today, for instance, I've got ham and cheese with mustard. Yesterday it was meat loaf with mustard."

It was blessedly cool in the shade, and would've been a serene picnic had it not been for the conversation.

"You wouldn't happen to remember, from last week, a fellow came in and returned a book," Pinnie said. "The Union High School stop. His book was out on interlibrary loan. It had *North American Indian* in the title. I've got a record of it, of course, me being professional, everything neat and clean and in its own place. This fellow got a notice from the main library that the book was still overdue. He wasn't too happy about this and telephoned the library to lodge a complaint. The downtown library can't seem to locate the book. And I've looked high and low in the book-mobile—no luck. Now, I've given this some thought, and here's the conclusion I've come to. I can either hire Sherlock Holmes to solve this mystery or just get it over with and pay full price for the book out of pocket, seeing its disappearance happened on my watch. How would you advise me here?"

Basically, I confessed all my crimes by indirection—that is, by trying to blame someone else. "Now I remember the book," I said.

"It was about how to trap wild birds. So, what I think is that the man from the Union High stop is the one who killed the swan in the newspaper."

"Interesting theory, Sherlock."

"Which Sherlock Holmes should I start with, do you think?"

"*Hound of the Baskervilles.* Without a moment's hesitation, *Hound of the Baskervilles.*"

"Okay, I'll start with that one, then."

"How many interlibrary return forms do you think you've filled out so far this summer, give or take?"

"I don't know."

"Take a wild guess."

"Maybe a hundred."

"Say, in theory, you were to screw up just one time out of that hundred. I'd bet most anyone would chalk that up to normal human error, don't you think? I mean, I've fallen asleep in church more times out of a hundred than that. Nobody's perfect."

"I'll try and think of it that way from now on."

"Look, I don't mean to sound like I'm giving fatherly advice, mind you. You already have a father. But return that goddamn book, okay?" He cuffed the top of my head hard and said, "What expression do you see on my face right now?"

"I can't read it."

"Disappointment, that's what."

The next day during lunch, I put *North American Indian Waterfowl Traps, Weirs, and Snares* on top of the card catalogue, filled out the proper interlibrary return form, and placed it like a bookmark in the book.

I hadn't meant to kill the swan. It was a beautiful, mean bird, and spent nights in my secret haunt. Nearly fifty years later, I can still hear its strange guttural exhalation; fifty years of hapless guilt and remorse. So often I close my eyes and picture the water closing over.

My fifteenth summer was ending. My older brother started to talk about enlisting in the army. This didn't go down well with Paris. "If Michael joins the army," she said, "I'll move to my namesake city and never speak to him again." But before he could make any decision, Michael first had to serve time in the Kent County Correctional Facility for car theft. His starting date was August 30.

The evening of August 29, he drove with Paris to Reeds Lake. How did I know this? Because I had driven to the lake myself, parked my car under a willow tree, and walked to the area where the love cars parked. Right away I heard my brother's inimitable fusillades of laughter. Then I heard "Sherry" by the Four Seasons—Paris half singing, half screaming, "Sher-er-ee, Sher-ee bay-yay-bee!" in a duet with Frankie Valli, whose every falsetto surge was like a shot of adrenaline administered to the radio. I saw a bottle of whiskey float the length of the back seat, as if levitating sideways. It was a very hot night, still around eighty degrees at nine p.m., which wasn't unusual that summer. Reeds Lake was famous for being one of the best make-out spots in the city. The police left the love cars alone. Nightly rendezvous there were necessary and beautiful—at least that's what I was led to understand, and I was led to understand it by Paris. "Now that you own a car," she once told me, "see how much you have to look forward to?"

I saw Paris's car. I saw her feet, with her favorite red high heels on; she wore those shoes no matter what the occasion, sometimes even first thing in the morning, going to the diner for breakfast. I could see her legs, wide apart, resting on the base of the open rear window, those red high heels somehow still balanced on her feet, suspended in the night air.

I stripped down to my swimsuit and slipped into the lake to cool off. At one point, when I looked up and saw dozens of gulls perched on the paddle wheeler, I clapped my hands loudly four or five times, and they flew off as though I'd rudely interrupted a conference of ghosts. They scattered every which way, out over the moon-in-a-mirror dark water, gone into stars.

"No more unscheduled stops necessary," Pinnie Oler said by way of announcing that Martha was pregnant. I had only two more days left to work in the bookmobile. I'd asked if I could keep after-school hours, but Pinnie said there was no money in the library budget for that. "Maybe next summer, huh?"

When the bookmobile stopped across from Dykstra's, I looked out and saw quite a commotion. There was a police car out front. I saw two policemen inside the apothecary, along with my father, Mr. Dykstra, his employee Marcelline, and Robert Boxer. One policeman waved the others to one side of the room. Then he put handcuffs on my father's wrists and led him out to the cruiser. My father got into the back seat. One policeman got in behind the wheel, the other rode shotgun. Pinnie said, "I'm going in and find out what happened." I watched through the bookmobile window. A few minutes later, when Pinnie returned, he said, "Looks like that fellow Larry reached into the cash register. Marcelline Vanderhook called the cops."

I slumped onto one of the benches. "But you know what Peter Dykstra said just now?" Pinnie continued. "He said, 'I'm not about to press charges on a war hero, fellow I've been talking and drinking coffee with every day for months who just got overcome by a desperate notion. Besides, I think this heat's made everyone go haywire. You'd almost have to have gone haywire to reach into a cash register like that.'"

So, I thought, my father had told everyone in the apothecary that he was a war hero.

And here is the last remembered truth of that summer. The next day, when we parked the bookmobile across from Dykstra's, my father was inside having coffee, as usual. I decided now was the time to walk in the door and set the record straight. Marcelline was there, and of course Mr. Dykstra. So was Robert Boxer, who was packaging up this and that item for delivery. WGRD was on the radio. I ordered a root beer. Robert introduced me to his dad. Peter Dykstra and I shook hands. I said, "Larry here is my father." Everyone but my father looked incredulous. "You let my father drive your Studebaker. That was nice of you."

Perhaps I should not admit this, but at the end of that summer I found it compelling and not peculiar to talk to ducks, gulls, even swans at a distance. After school started up again, I continued to go to Reeds Lake—through much of that unseasonably hot September, if memory serves. I'd swim around under the steamboat's paddle wheel. By talking to the birds I meant to reinstate each night an unthreatening familiarity. I could scarcely sleep because of my relentless sorrow over the dead swan. Simply put, it wasn't so much that I felt things any more deeply than anyone else, but that this was the thing I'd chosen to feel most deeply about. How unhinged this seems to me now, my murmuring and cooing and stuttering and imitating nighttime birds like that. What was wrong with me? And I had an inkling that my soul was off-kilter, askew, and that I was in a phase of moving away from people. I wasn't exactly afraid of this, only curious, and wanted to chronicle it. In late October, when the lake got too cold to swim in, and the ducks and swans had jettisoned my useless presence and apologies, migrating south in their formations, I remember feeling bereft.

GREY GEESE DESCENDING

⁓

M Y CANADIAN UNCLE, Isador, knew the actor Peter
Lorre. In fact, Lorre had arranged for a bit part in a
movie, *The Cross of Lorraine,* for Isador. And Isador insisted on
calling Lorre, a Hungarian Jew, by his original name. "If Laszlo
Lowenstein doesn't wish to acknowledge he's Jewish, that's his
professional choice," Isador said.

In September of 1969 I moved to Nova Scotia, because a
friend of mine was going to live in Amsterdam for a year and
said I could sublet his room in the Lord Nelson Hotel in Halifax
for thirty-five dollars a month. I had no prospects but this cheap
room. And that was enough to get me there.

I was adrift. Between graduating from high school in 1967 and
moving to Halifax in 1969, I had lived in Toronto, Ottawa, Berke-
ley, and Vancouver. As for employment, for eighteen months I
wrote pop music reviews for the *Interpreter,* an alternative news-
paper based in Grand Rapids. One of my assignments was to
cover a concert in Vancouver by Donovan, an immensely popular
Scottish singer and songwriter. The next assignment was to write

an article — my idea — about the Institute for the Study of Non-violence, in Palo Alto, California. To get from Vancouver to the institute, I purchased a jeep for $350 and began to drive south. It was my first time on the West Coast. I stopped in Inverness and Point Reyes Station, California, where I stayed for a dollar a night in a kind of fisherman's shack at the end of a dock jutting into Bodega Bay. Under the dock, ducks found shelter from the rain. Pelicans were a constant presence. By the time I had walked three trails at the Point Reyes National Seashore, I had planned to return there.

When I finished my article on the Institute for the Study of Nonviolence, having met its two founders, Joan Baez and Ira Sandperl — the most enthralling intellect I'd ever met — my antiwar convictions solidified. Yet when I left Palo Alto I still felt unsettled. I spent the summer in a cottage in Jeffersonville, New York, a twenty-five-minute drive from Max Yasgur's farm and the Woodstock festival. I attended this monumental event. At the end of that summer, my only goal was the cheap hotel room in Halifax.

So I found myself in a Canadian city that I was determined to know better. I also had designs on writing radio plays for the CBC. I thought I would trace one family's story from their fleeing Hitler's persecution to their arrival through immigration at Halifax's Pier 21 — a major port of entry for refugees — and their subsequent life in the city. I had outlined a ten-part drama on this subject, but I'd never written for radio before. Truth be told, I simply wanted to be able to say to someone, "I write for radio." Just that sentence gave me inspiration, as fatuous as it may sound. In fact, I'd seen a CBC advertisement for "auditions," which meant you could send in a radio play and they would decide whether to use it or not. I was twenty; it all seemed like a good idea at the time. It was my only idea at the time.

For a few evenings now I've been listening to the jazz pianist Joe Sealy's record *Africville Suite*. Sealy's father was born in the section of Halifax known as Africville. Sealy himself was working there at the time of the unspeakable "relocation" of the mostly black community during the years 1964 through 1967, and he composed the *Africville Suite* in memory of his father. My girlfriend Mathilde Kamal's mother was also raised in Africville. I've been thinking about the last conversation I had with Mathilde, two days before her four-passenger charter plane, subjected to blizzard conditions and possibly pilot error, slammed to the frozen ground in Saskatchewan—the bleak winter landscape that was the exclusive subject of her latest watercolors.

Mathilde was twenty-six when I met her. She was worldly, and I was a pin stuck in a street map of Halifax, at 416 Morris Street, my address that autumn and into the winter of 1970. Too often self-deprecation can be a form of self-regard: *I'm nothing—praise me.* To my mind, self-deprecation is useless except when it is used as the first rung on a ladder of self-reckoning. Once at a restaurant, before we ordered dinner, when I'd lamented the great differences in our educations and experiences—"Mathilde, after all, you've lived all over Europe!"—she tapped her wine glass with a spoon as if about to offer a toast. "Distasteful way of thinking, my friend," she said. "You are what you are. I love you. Now let's order. I'm very hungry."

But by any standard, Mathilde *was* worldly. She was born in Morocco of a French father and a Canadian mother—her parents had moved to Morocco the year before Mathilde's birth. She was educated at the Sorbonne, had exhibitions of her work in London and Bruges, and had been married for a year to a much older man, a museum curator in Amsterdam. After finalizing her divorce, she moved to Halifax, where she lived in a shabby two-room apartment on Robie Street near Citadel Park. "I moved to Halifax because the Nova Scotia College of Art and Design offered me a course to teach," she told me once. "I wasn't good at it. But it paid the rent and I liked the city. So here I am."

The moment we met, in early September 1969 in a café on Hollis Street, I was attracted to her, but not in a head-over-heels way. I think she sensed this, and it put her at ease. Mathilde had, as she put it, "suffered adoration" in her life. She often spoke autobiographically, but seldom confessionally. When she was nineteen, her future husband had pursued her, which she emphatically said bored her to tears. "Because men look, doesn't mean you look back." She had aphorisms about such things; some were more convincing than others.

During the first months of our courtship, it was almost entirely a matter of her fixing on me her affection and commitment. She did this with her eyes wide open, with full agency, and without compromise, and because it pleased her. She wanted life to be different, so she made it different. This, for the first time in my life, made me feel attractive, but it was because she intensified the attractiveness of life, and drew me into that. It was like being invited into a philosophy. I wasn't passive, I was just riding a strong wave. She had purpose. She had talent and flair. She liked to quote some movie or other in a defiant, Bette Davis voice: "Like I said, I don't quake when things get tough, and I don't make deals with the devil." I was what might be called a work in progress; Mathilde already had definite refinements and opinions enough to fill a thick volume. Her opinions always struck me as born of experience, but of course they couldn't all have been.

With Mathilde I was taken by surprise, grateful, but resistant, questioning, and vigilant about complications—and then slowly, painstakingly, I realized I was indeed head over heels. We held hands everywhere. One summer day I called her darling. This just flew out; it was not a word I'd heard used by my parents, nor had I ever used it myself. (I'd heard it in the movies.) Mathilde used it often and freely. She said it with feeling. It all seemed a lot to fit into less than a year's time. Then Mathilde was gone.

Mathilde first exhibited her work in 1967, part of a group show in a warehouse space in north London. I saw only photographs of the paintings: eight works in oil that were as far in aesthetics, style, and subject matter from her future watercolor landscapes as could possibly be imagined. For one thing, the early paintings were full of people; her final landscapes not only had no people in them, but the settings suggested that people had never lived in them.

Her part of the London exhibit was called "Memories of Africville." The title referred to her mother's memories and to things Mathilde had discovered while doing library research. To the extent that these paintings comprised a cumulative portrait of hardscrabble life in Africville, there was a near-documentary immediacy to them. Mathilde, at that young age, used paint in a way she herself said was influenced by Chaim Soutine, whose paintings she'd studied in Paris, where Soutine had lived. "Paint put on thickly, emotion put on thickly," she explained. "Even his trees are emotional." She made portraits of black seamen, Pullman porters, domestic servants. She painted meetings of the African Baptist

Association and local churches. There were three paintings of the Africville prison. One work depicted a solid-waste facility built to take the filth of a neighboring town, another showed people scavenging for clothes and lengths of copper pipe in a garbage dump. There was a painting of children in an infectious-disease hospital.

When referring to these documentary works, Mathilde was measured if not dismissive. "I don't regret painting them. It felt like I was saying to my mother, I know where you come from. But I gave every last painting away. Finally they felt more like an obligation, things I was supposed to paint. Nothing wrong with that, but I couldn't paint out of obligation anymore, pure and simple. But don't tell me life isn't strange. Who could've predicted, the first time I went out there, the effect Saskatchewan would have on me? It was like my soul had new eyes. I felt my soul come alive. Like in my past life, I was actually part of that landscape. I thought, Now I'm me, present-day Mathilde, but painting my former self. That's probably kind of Buddhist."

"We should elope," Mathilde said. We were walking on Water Street near Historic Properties. "I've always wanted the experience of eloping."

"Elope to where?" I asked.

"I was thinking Saskatchewan."

"Knowing you," I said, "you'd want to get married standing out on some godforsaken prairie."

"Godforsaken?" she said. "I don't think that's true at all. I find God out there."

"An abundance of churches doesn't necessarily mean hospitality."

"What's bugging you? Is it our age difference again? The age difference bothers you a lot, doesn't it? Let me put it this way. I've already tried older. Now I'm trying younger."

For whatever reason, hearing herself utter this made Mathilde double over in laughter. Other pedestrians out in the bitter cold that day stared at us. Then, as if by some telepathic communication, we both noticed we were standing in front of a small art gallery. Wordlessly we agreed to go inside. It had begun to snow. The gallery was nearly empty. Tea, hot cocoa, wine, cheese, and crackers were laid out on a long table. Mathilde was immediately drawn to a painting called *Grey Geese Descending*. I got two paper cups of cocoa and joined her.

Grey Geese Descending was about twenty-four inches wide and eighteen inches high, and showed five grey geese about to alight on a pond. Their wings were spread to slow and balance their gliding descent. One appeared to be mishandling its approach, its body slightly contorted, its feathers decidedly more ruffled than the others', as if its flight through the mountain pass and valley in the background had been more harrowing, as though the gods of travel themselves had put up resistance.

Mathilde stepped back and pointed to the disheveled goose. "See, that's what happens when it got confused."

"I had no idea you could read the minds of Japanese geese."

"I never told you that?" She was keeping things light.

"Melancholy day, isn't it?" I said. "In the painting, I mean. Overcast sky and everything."

"Geese may not get sad about the same things you get sad about. Besides, overcast skies are better to see birds by. Haven't you noticed that?"

"Yes, I have."

"I mean, you love to go out and look at birds over at Port Medway, and even at the harbor here in the city, right? I like to

47

see crows against the grey skies out in Saskatchewan. Then there's my seagulls everywhere that I love so much. That's something we truly have in common, right? That and things that go on with us under the quilt. Tell me, do you like this painting or not?"

I said, "You make decisions, like or dislike, faster than me."

We looked at all the paintings and some scrolls, drank hot chocolate and wine, and ate cheese and crackers, everything that was on offer. It was our dinner. We were in the gallery for about half an hour, I'd say. Then we repaired to a student café on Duke Street near the Nova Scotia College of Art and Design. We took a window-side table. When our espressos arrived, Mathilde said, "I'll elope with you if we can come to some agreement on the painting we just saw. And don't act like you're merely resigned to talking about this. I want you to be interested."

Just then, for all her insistence, as she sat across the wooden table from me, her coat and scarf still on, I got lost in her physical self — *entranced* might be the word — as if I were memorizing her. This no doubt doesn't speak well for me: shouldn't one live fully in the moment? Still, there it was. Barely shoulder-length black hair with two red streaks swirled up in a topknot and tucked under her knitted hat, skin flushed from the cold, brown eyes wistful even when she was joyful, prominent cheekbones, and her nose — which, as she had put it, "I only liked after it was broken when I was playing high school lacrosse," and which had been broken a second time when she'd taken a spill from a moped. She had a slightly tilted smile that thrilled me.

Almost without reprieve, we had been out of sync with each other, contentious, all without discussion, for about a week. The most vexing aspect of this was to experience the symptoms of Mathilde's discontent without knowing if there was an exact cause. She'd been painting for upward of eighteen hours a day. I hadn't discovered a passion even remotely comparable. I liked to read and look at birds and compose long handwritten letters. But I sensed that *liking* wasn't enough to fill a life.

"Where are you?" she asked.

"Sorry, I drifted off."

"We should talk about the painting. I think we saw it differently."

We sat there until the café closed, which must've been midnight at least. *Grey Geese Descending* was ostensibly the subject at hand. But for the next few hours deeper information about each other was also being requisitioned. Hard to describe this, but I believe we both knew something was ending. Then, either you have to start a second romance within the first or all is lost. More likely, Mathilde knew it, and I didn't want to know it. After her death, I understood that by presenting the offer—"I'll elope with you if we can come to some agreement on the painting"—she might have intended it as a kind of fait accompli, since she knew in advance that we would not agree. To put it another way, if in the end this conversation wasn't intended to be a kind of elegy, each sentence we spoke seemed tense with elegiac anticipation. Half an hour into it I wanted the conversation to stop, and Mathilde seemed about to ask the café's proprietor to let us stay the entire night in order to continue it.

I thought *Grey Geese Descending*, in every specific and general aspect, was an allegory of sadness; conversely, Mathilde saw it as having captured "the mood of the painter and therefore the mood of the landscape itself." She said, "You don't really know enough about psychology to psychologize so much about this painting. That kind of talk keeps you from feeling the beauty of it."

I said, "You're the one who tried to tell me what that goose was thinking—that it was hesitating to land."

"Stop reading yourself into the painting."

On and on like that. It would have been wonderful if we were simply using different sensibilities to come to a mutual understanding, a duet of opposite natures, but this was more an exchange, in self-consciously subdued voices, of a maddening civility that might more characterize the first conversation between two people trying to get to know each other. Then, minutes before the café closed, Mathilde asked with huffy directness, "Did you realize that my saying we should elope was a marriage proposal?" I said, "But since you didn't invite me to Saskatchewan . . . " Mathilde said, "We can elope right here in Halifax."

Using a directory and the café's telephone, we woke up a justice of the peace at one a.m. and walked to his house. After a few perfunctory questions, he said, "This can't legally work. You, sir, are an American citizen, and you, madam, are a citizen of Morocco. Also, you need a witness." Mathilde said, "We can be our own witnesses." "Not on paper," the justice of the peace said. We shrugged, apologized for waking him but not for the reason we had woken him, and left, acquiescing for the moment to international legalities.

Within an hour, in bed in Mathilde's apartment, our uninhibited lovemaking was new and surprising. Something had let go. "I don't care what anybody says. This feels like a marriage bed," she said, then got up to smoke a cigarette and make coffee.

"Well, you'd know and I wouldn't."

I immediately regretted saying that, but she seemed to ignore it. Yet the very sweat on our bodies and bedclothes seemed to be the prescient fragrance of final melancholy. Our lips were sore and swollen, and we took separate hot baths.

The next morning, Mathilde left before I woke, two days earlier than she'd originally planned. From Regina, Saskatchewan, she sent a picture postcard of a man and woman eloping: the man had set a ladder against a house and was standing on the top rung, just outside the woman's open bedroom window, through which she was handing him her suitcase. Through the living room window you could see the woman's mother and father watching television. President Eisenhower was on the screen. There was a full moon in the sky. The scolding caption read: *The moon makes these two act impetuously! Big mistake!* Matilda's own handwritten message was: *I do.*

I don't know much about premonition. Nor would I necessarily recognize, let alone trust, its opportunities. Yet thinking back on those particular days, it may have been some sort of premonitory agitation that kept me awake for the eight nights of Hanukkah, which framed on the calendar Mathilde's absence. I slept in fits and starts during the day, but I didn't sleep one minute at night. It was an insomnia tailored to this circumstance and was unnerving.

Isador Sarovnik wasn't technically my uncle. I informally adopted him and referred to him as an uncle because, beyond his being avuncular, I felt far closer to him than I did to any of my actual relatives. Bereft of parents, bereft of locatable uncles and aunts, I began to concentrate every ounce of filial love and affection onto others, Isador being the most indispensable and dear to me.

In Isador I saw the complete résumé of an interesting, beloved uncle. In December of 1969, Isador was eighty-one years old. He had retired at age sixty-five from being a bellman ("I was the first Jewish senior bellman in Nova Scotia, possibly in all of Canada") at several hotels in Halifax, ending with the Lord Nelson. Before Hitler's psychotic Reich, Isador had been a stage actor in Berlin and Budapest; as he mentioned at every opportunity, as a young man he was friends with Peter Lorre. "Lazzy got me a little acting work after the war," Isador told me. Given that all but a few of his relatives, and many of his friends, had been slaughtered in concentration camps, the fact that Isador had played, in *The Cross of Lorraine*, the part of a Nazi soldier was something he could never forgive himself for, "even though I was raising a family and needed work." His wife, Sarah, had died in 1962, and his two daughters lived in Vancouver; he saw them infrequently, which was a source of great sadness to him.

Isador harbored special affection for Peter Lorre, and once, quite seriously, said to me, "In the 1950s I wrote a letter to Los Angeles and invited Lazzy to Halifax, but he had no interest in this part of the world. I would have made it nice for him. Rolled out the red carpet in the hotel here. Too bad." One night in his hotel room I watched *Casablanca* with Isador. When Lorre first appeared onscreen, Isador said, "Lazzy looks very good in that suit."

When Hanukkah arrived, Isador asked me to eat dinner with him on all eight nights in his room, number 411. By then I knew the hotel. I'd had short-lived employment as a bellman at a time when Isador, a respected emeritus figure, was filling in as concierge for a man who had the flu. I remember Isador saying, "I call it influenza—not flu. You don't use nicknames. You don't buddy up to something that can kill you." As a bellman I'd lasted about ten days, finally getting sacked because I called a woman whose luggage I was carrying a "wrinkled fucking old whore" in response to her confiding to me in the electric lift, "I wouldn't have registered in this hotel had I known an old Jew was the concierge." As it happened, the manager of the hotel had been in the electric lift, too.

I delivered the suitcases to the woman's room. Every bellman had been instructed to tell each patron his name and say, "If there is anything you need, please ask for me at the front desk." But after setting her suitcases down, I said, "If you want to jump out the window, call the front desk and ask for me. I'll come right up and open it for you." I didn't wait for a tip. The hotel manager had politely kept the gate of the electric lift open and was waiting for me. I was unemployed by the time we reached the lobby.

Despite being fired, I often hung around the hotel lobby. I liked sitting on one of the big sofas to read. I had lunch with Isador at least three times a week. But the pertinent thing here is that Isador adored Mathilde. I knew so few people in Halifax, and he was the one person who spent any time with us as a couple, mainly over dinners at the hotel. On the other hand, I met any number of Mathilde's artist friends, usually over coffee in cafés or at art galleries. Whenever anyone asked me what I did in life, I'd say, "I'm working on it"—feeble, unimpressive, but true. Once, a little tipsy at a painting exhibit, I said, "Well, I'm going to write a novel, but I'm not starting it for fifteen years." (This must have sounded acerbic if not delusional, but as it turned out, it was prophetic: my first novel was published when I was thirty-eight, and it took three years to write.) I knew the question, from Mathilde's friends, was really, "Why are you with him?" It was a good question, a question from curious and protective friends. It was a question I'd often asked myself.

So, during Hanukkah, Isador would say the blessings, light the candles, and set out dinner, sent up from the hotel kitchen. I had some deep discussions with him about life and love. By *life* I mean Mathilde. With Isador it was never a case of his dishing out platitudes, no *Tuesdays with Morrie* bullshit, all sweetness and light. "You know who I saw the other day?" he asked. "That son of a bitch Mr. Kelb. You remember, I told you he used to live in the hotel here, what, maybe twenty years. Then his son and daughter-in-law gave him his own room above their garage. Do you know that when that son of a bitch lived in the hotel, he used to walk in, hand me his bag of groceries — me, the senior bellman — get on the electric lift, and slide the gate shut behind him so I'd have to wait for him to send it down again. He'd say the same goddamn thing every time: 'I prefer to go upstairs unencumbered.' Let them put that on his gravestone for all I care. Except I hope when he kicks the bucket he's going downstairs, not upstairs, if you know what I mean."

Apart from the elopement postcard, I wasn't hearing from Mathilde at all. On the fifth night of Hanukkah, I mentioned this to Isador. He'd just set the room service tray out in the hallway. "What's there for her to tell you?" Isador said. "She's freezing her *tuches* off out there in Saskatchewan. She's painting her paintings. She's sleeping, she's waking up. But that's not the problem, is it? No, the problem is, you're in over your head with this Mathilde. You're drowning. She's walking so far ahead of you — is this how it feels? — she's about to turn the corner and disappear. You need to figure out what skills you have. I can get you work in the hotel if you want. I'm sure the thing that happened with the anti-Semite is water under the bridge by now. Besides, the hotel's got a new owner. It's been advertising for bellmen."

"I showed Mathilde some of my writing."

"What did she say about it?"

"She suggested hotel work — for the time being."

"See, brilliant minds think alike. There's worse things than hotel work, let me remind you."

Each night a candle was added to the menorah on Isador's kitchen table; each night another conversation about the ongoing soap opera, as Isador called my life. By the eighth night, he'd narrowed his tolerance for my unwillingness to see the truth. "Once and for all, here's my understanding of everything with this," he said. "Your Mathilde's got bigger appetites for life than you have. God in heaven, you can't even read half the same menu she's reading. So what's your choice? Savor the time you have with this Mathilde, for as long as one of *her* appetites is for you. Count your blessings. Let me put this in an old immigrant's way: she's got a lot of stickers on her steamer trunk." (I've never since been able to see, in a photograph or movie, world travelers about to embark on, say, a 1930s luxury liner, standing on the dock next to their big steamer trunks festooned with travel stickers, without thinking of Isador saying this to me.) "Now, can we *please* try and enjoy the last night of this ancient holiday without you sounding like such a pitiful shmuck? *Meshuggeh,* so worked up! It's like you've forgotten how to take a piss. Forgotten how to lift a fork to your mouth. You aren't thinking of doing anything harmful to yourself, are you?"

Roughly a month after I'd first met Mathilde, I got Isador to go with me to my favorite birding haunt near Port Medway, about a two-hour drive from Halifax. This was, believe me, a triumph of Herculean dimensions, getting Isador Sarovnik out to a beach. Through stubborn persistence I'd managed to persuade the editor of the travel section of the Sunday *Halifax Herald* to commission an article on a protected bird preserve. I felt this to be the start of something substantial, possibly even a career. Once I'd informed Isador and asked him to accompany me, he said, "Sure, why not? I'd just as soon drop dead out by the Atlantic Ocean as anywhere, what's the difference? Besides, I need the actual evidence of you earning some money, being a solid citizen. You can take your millions and buy your Mathilde some paintbrushes. How much are they paying you, this newspaper, to write about birds?"

It was $150, but the way I put it was, "Over three months' worth of rent."

It was early October, warm and windy on the rocky beach. "This is Canada," Isador said. "Winter can arrive suddenly, on a whim. So I'm wearing more layers than a layer cake." He had napped on the drive out. I sat him down in a folding chair out of the wind, between boulders, facing the sea. I stuck an umbrella fixed to a long pole in the sand, supplied him with water and lemonade, a makeshift oasis.

"I have mixed feelings about the ocean," he said when he had settled in. "Some days I have real affection for it. Other days I feel otherwise." I walked back and forth along the beach, taking notes on what late-staying sea and shore birds I could find, checking identifications against my field guide. When I got back to Isador, he said, "I've been thinking. Now that we're out here, can you arrange for a nice duck for supper? I'm in good standing with the hotel chef."

"Maybe next time," I said. "I'm going to sit with you for a while, then I have to walk to the marsh—that's the actual place I'm commissioned to write about. Are you going to be all right?"

"You put too much sugar in the lemonade," he said. "You know, I look at the ocean and I think, I never learned to swim. Lucky thing I didn't fall off the boat that brought me to Canada. Some people, and I saw this with my own eyes, jumped off the ship halfway between there and here. No matter how bad things had gotten for them before, they figured it was going to get worse."

"You don't know all the reasons, Isador."

"I'm only saying, I saw it with my own eyes."

I sat drinking lemonade with him, talking about this and that.

"This is a comfortable chair you provided for me here," he said. "If I ever get to go on an ocean cruise, I'd like this chair. Do they let you bring your own chairs?"

"I don't know."

"Coming over from Europe, that's not what I'd call an ocean cruise."

"No, I guess not, Isador."

"I had a change of clothing and my childhood menorah. That's it."

"You told me."

"That was a rough passage. Nobody knew their fates. Nobody knew what was what. What was this place Canada, anyway? Still, Jewish children from many countries were conceived on shipboard those weeks. How anyone found privacy on that ship beats me. A hotel, now that's a different story. But a ship full of refugees—really something, don't you think?"

"Yes, I do. Would you like to get back to the city now?"

"You said you had more you needed to look at."

"I can come back, if you're too tired."

"In a little while. This umbrella is nice. Let me ask you something. What's with you and birds, anyway? I don't understand."

"I look at those sea ducks and I wonder where they go at the end of a day."

"What's the mystery? At the end of the day they go home. What's there to figure out?"

"Want to look at sea ducks through these binoculars? They have beautiful faces."

"I prefer the pigeons of my Russian youth. I close my eyes and see them. For this I don't need binoculars."

"I'll be back in an hour, probably. No more than two."

Later that October, Mathilde and I drove out to Peggy's Cove, mainly to walk on the beach, catch the last autumn sun, and have lunch at the Oyster Café. In the car, I offered the fact of my having been at the Woodstock music festival back in August as a bona fide of worldliness. This didn't have the effect I'd hoped for. Mathilde listened intently, as focused as a stenographer who would be responsible for reading back a transcript, as I described what I'd seen and heard in the muddy fields and hills of Yasgur's upstate New York property. I dropped the names of musicians, some of whom I saw perform: Janis Joplin, Jimi Hendrix, the Incredible String Band, Richie Havens, Canned Heat, the Who, Joan Baez, and Crosby, Stills, Nash & Young. I mentioned that I saw a lot of people making love on rubber rafts on a pond. I told her I had the use of a cottage in Jeffersonville, not far from the festival site, owned by the poet Jerome Rothenberg and his wife, Diane, in dairy farm country.

When I had finished my recollections, Mathilde, between kissing my ears and mouth with big smacking noises and mussing my hair, all teasing sweetness, interrogated me, hoping to discover to what extent I'd authentically experienced things at Woodstock. "So you probably had a bath every night," she said, "at your friend's cozy little cottage, right? Did you have any luck in the fucking-in-the-pond department? Did you get hypnotized by what's-his-face, the Maharishi-something? Did you get all crazy and slide on your bare ass in the mud? You tell me, but my guess is, no to all of the above."

"I had a very good time listening to the music," I said. "Mostly

I sat on a hill way back from the stage and looked at the performers through binoculars. Is that what you wanted to hear?"

"Oh, I've hurt your feelings."

"No, it's just that I thought I'd had a better time than I obviously did."

Mathilde attempted a reconciliation. She held my hand in hers and said, "If I were there, I'd have wanted to sit in that bathtub with you. I don't need a pond. I prefer a bed. I'm glad you had a nice time."

"In my own way."

"You know what the joke is about Woodstock? Because of all the dope and LSD and stuff? The joke is, if you remember Woodstock, you weren't really there."

"So then, by those lights, I wasn't there. But still I remember it."

The plane had departed Regina at dusk and lost radio contact somewhere between the airport and Kyle, in north-central Saskatchewan province. The wreckage was found scattered and smoldering. Mathilde had been the only passenger. She always scrupulously worked out a strict budget for her painting sojourns; transportation was always the most difficult part to afford. The pilot's and her bodies were incinerated; Mathilde's identity was forensically verified by dental records. The inventory of possessions in her motel room in Kyle included toiletries, canvases, paintbrushes and tubes of paint, turpentine, postcards, a book of watercolors by Toulouse-Lautrec, and a book of watercolors by Egon Schiele. Her remains and her paintings were sent to London; she was buried there within walking distance of her parents' townhouse. When I wrote to extend my condolences, Mathilde's mother's return note read: "Thank you. Although we did not know any of you, it is a comfort to know that Mathilde had so many Canadian friends."

The trajectory of a life sponsored for any period by unresolved conversations and love, and then abruptly deprived of these things, is something to behold, let alone experience firsthand. In the immediate aftermath of Mathilde's death I did a number of things without rhyme or reason, but perhaps with what the poet Denise Levertov called, in a lecture I heard her give, "the marionetting of the whole person by an invisible hand, the sorrow dance." Whoever or whatever was in control of my life over the next six or so months, it wasn't me. Quite often I'd simply fall off a curb.

Amid this disorderly order of psychological incidents, as I have come to think of them, I decided to take Isador up on his offer to get me work at the Lord Nelson Hotel. He had given me a magazine article titled "Hold Your Tongue," which contained advice about how to know when a person should, and shouldn't, keep his opinion to himself. I had a low opinion of this article. But Isador said, "It's useful for a bellman." He had set up an interview with the personnel director of the hotel. I put on my dark brown herringbone sports coat, black trousers, beige shirt, necktie, and black dress shoes, and arrived early for my two p.m. interview.

As soon as I stepped into the lobby, however, I noticed two young women carrying a painting of tropical birds, walking toward a conference room down a hallway off the lobby. I followed them and discovered that an auction was in progress. I knew that on occasion private auctions were held in the hotel. This one dealt primarily with eighteenth- and nineteenth-century zoological and botanical book illustrations, and a few other drawings and paintings as well. There were approximately forty people in attendance, along with the auctioneer and his staff. I sat in the back row as if I'd been invited.

Looking around, I saw that I was properly dressed for this auction. I sat through the bidding for half a dozen works. I sensed a certain acquisitive fever in the air, but by and large the auction was all etiquette and protocol, and for me every moment was an education. People were forking over impressive sums of money, upward of five thousand dollars for a drawing, which to me was an unimaginable amount. Then an eighteenth-century work, *Laughing Gull,* painted by Mark Catesby, was put on the easel, and the bidding started. I cannot say what got into me, but when the auctioneer reached the point of asking, "Do I hear three thousand?" I shot my arm in the air like a schoolboy excitedly wanting to answer a question. At that time I had around eighty dollars in my savings account.

I was startled when the auctioneer addressed me directly. "Sir, are you representing yourself?"

"Yes," I said.

"Very well," he said. "We have a bid of three thousand. Do I hear three thousand five hundred?"

A woman in the front row held up a kind of paddle. The auctioneer said, "We have thirty-five hundred. Mark Catesby, first reproduction of the original for portfolio—*Laughing Gull.* Provenance fully verified. Do I hear four thousand?"

"Four thousand!" I said.

"Four thousand once. Four thousand twice. Sold—for four thousand dollars."

Not to mention the commission due the auction house.

I'd missed my interview. Isador was not pleased. I found him playing checkers with the chef in the restaurant's kitchen. The

chef said, "I'll leave you two alone to talk. I've got dinner to pre-
pare, eh?"

I sat down across a table from Isador and told him about the
auction. "Did you sign legal papers?" he asked. "Did you put your
John Henry on a bill of sale?"

"It was part of things."

"Then you're screwed—pardon my French."

"It just happened."

"You and birds. What did you buy again? A seagull?"

"An eighteenth-century seagull."

"That's been dead a long time."

"Isador!"

"Did Mathilde like seagulls? I'm asking."

"I'd say they were among her favorites."

"Okay, that explains some of it, but not the whole *meshuggeneh*
stupidity."

"I don't have the money to pay for it."

"Visiting hours probably will be on Thursdays and Saturdays,
and I promise not to fail you in that department. I'll bring you
lemon cake, your favorite. But I won't hide a saw in the cake, like
in the movies."

"This is no joke, Izzy."

"No, I should say it isn't. Look, go in there and tell them it was
a mistake. They can't get blood from a stone. You just don't have
the money. The problem is, once you win a bid, the thing's off the
market. Plus, you signed your name. This is not good."

"I'm screwed."

"You need employment."

The auction house was sympathetic, but legally unyielding. In
short, we worked out reparations. I would give them five hundred
dollars on the twentieth of each month until the debt was paid.

I signed another document to that effect. I was asked whether I wanted to return *Laughing Gull* and let the auction house privately advertise its availability. This would save us all embarrassment. If someone was interested at four thousand dollars, I'd be off the hook. I should have leaped at this opportunity, but I refused it. They kept the painting in storage.

Nearly broke, in debt up to my ears, I then made another lunatic decision, which was to rent Mathilde's vacant apartment on Robie Street. "So, you couldn't bring yourself to live with her before—not that she didn't ask," Isador summarized. "So now what? You'll live without her in the rooms you should've lived with her?"

"Actually, it's five dollars a month cheaper than my room is now."

"See it how you wish," he said.

I paid the landlord fifty dollars for the first month's rent, plus a twenty-five-dollar security deposit, which left me with five dollars in the bank. "Look," Isador said one evening—he was providing me dinner at the hotel; meat loaf, mashed potatoes, asparagus, a small salad, pie for dessert—"you're just twenty and already your nerves are shot. Try to put your ducks in a row, seeing as how you like birds so much—go out and get a job. Just promise me one thing, all right? Don't live alone with that seagull on the wall. Get a nice colorful quilt. I'll give you a typewriter from hotel storage. Type up some ideas and try to sell them to the newspaper again. Why not? Any luck with radio writing?"

"Not yet."

We ate and had some laughs. Isador said, "Guess what's on the TV at eight o'clock? *The Maltese Falcon.* Want to watch it?" So we settled down in Isador's small living room and watched *The Maltese Falcon,* with Peter Lorre playing a character named

Joel Cairo. "He is sinister in this one," Isador said. "My feeling about that strange voice Lazzy always used is that as an actor his soul was without portfolio. Because just try and figure out which country he's from, from the accent."

It's probably accurate to state that Isador was a kind of self-taught scholar of Peter Lorre's life and films. I don't mean he used scholarly words to describe any of it. But he knew a lot, especially about what he called Lorre's "early years." He didn't much care about movie stars, though like anyone he had his favorite movies. I was impressed by Isador's knowledge in these matters. When you don't know anything about a subject, everything's a revelation. "You ever watch the one called *M*?" he asked. "In that picture Lazzy murders a child. Talk about guilt! You don't get guiltier than Lazzy in that picture. There's nothing worse than murdering a child, is there? There's one scene, well, it's famous, I suppose. Lazzy looks into a mirror and twists his face all up. Like he wants to permanently change his features. His character hates himself. At least that's how I always see it."

Before I knew it, Isador's face—no, his entire posture, it seemed—fell into severe despondency. As if all his years had actual weight that was pressing on his shoulders, he slumped on the sofa and tears filled his eyes. He opened a bottle of vodka, poured us each a glass. Then he used one of his favorite phrases, which characterized his inventive locutions in Yiddish-accented English—*unconditional unforgiveness*. "I have unconditional unforgiveness toward myself," Isador said, pouring himself a second shot. "You understand what I refer to?"

"I was worried this would come up, Isador. Watching this movie."

"Just now I'm suffering plural remorses. Maybe you should go home."

Plural remorses—another of his memorable phrases.

But I didn't return to my apartment, which was Mathilde's former apartment. I stayed and heard Isador out yet again about his decision to play a Nazi in *The Cross of Lorraine*. Naturally, to anyone else this would comprise the tiniest footnote in film history. But in Isador's mind, it not only loomed large, it defined him from that point on as "not a good person."

Peter Lorre's and Isador's lives first intersected in the 1920s. Back then, in Germany and Austria, Lorre appeared in stage works by Bertolt Brecht; Isador was an understudy to him in *Mann Ist Mann*. He remembered going to a performance of the infamous musical *Happy End*, written by Brecht with music composed by Kurt Weill, and was friends for a few years with the actor Oskar Homolka. Isador and Lorre would meet in cafés in Berlin. "After Fritz Lang cast Lazzy in *M*—that was 1931—our lives fell away from each other almost completely. Then Hitler." In 1933 Isador traveled on a Dutch passport—"this cost me an arm and a leg"—to Amsterdam. He eventually entered Canada through Pier 21 in Halifax—"the Ellis Island of Canada," as he and many others referred to it. "I had dreams still of working on the stage, but in Halifax at that time there wasn't much opportunity." So began his work in hotels.

"As for my nemesis, *The Cross of Lorraine*," he said, "let me put it this way: for a moment it was a blessing, a paycheck, then the curse of a lifetime."

I had the pressing obligation to work off the debt for *Laughing Gull*, and two days after I'd purchased it at auction, I sat at the table in the cramped kitchen where Mathilde had served me breakfast and dinner. ("My opinion? If a woman doesn't at least sometimes cook meals for you to eat together, she doesn't love you. I don't care if it's just using a skillet on a hot plate," she'd said after making lamb chops in a skillet on a hot plate.) I was scouring the employment listings in the *Halifax Herald*.

My eye caught an advertisement for a night janitor at Nova Scotia Hospital on Dartmouth Street. I had a perfunctory interview with the director of maintenance services. She asked two questions: did I have a criminal record, and did I mind working alone. I signed some employment and tax forms, and she said, "You can start tomorrow night. Report to Mr. McKenzie in the cafeteria at nine o'clock. Your hours are nine p.m. to six a.m., and you don't work on Friday or Saturday nights, but Sunday you work."

The next night, Mr. McKenzie, who was about sixty and the size of the actor Sydney Greenstreet, showed me the ropes. He introduced me to the men and women of the night janitorial staff and gave me a tour of the hospital wards, the supply rooms, the emergency exits. His instructions in how to use the electric floor polisher came with a World War Two reference. "I ran mine sweepers along the beaches in France," he said, demonstrating the polisher. "Now you try it." The machine was surprisingly difficult to control; in my first attempt, along a corridor in the children's ward, it ricocheted loudly off the floorboards, leaving black scuff marks. "You'll have to scrub those off," he said. "You've just made extra work for yourself." Then Mr. McKenzie left me to practice with the floor polisher.

My first night of official employment I polished eight corridors on three different floors, and as a result my shoulder and arm muscles, my lower back and calves, felt knotted and sore. When Mr. McKenzie checked on me at about midnight, he said, "There's muscle liniment in your locker. Don't go asking a nurse to rub it in, either. The nurses'll kick your butt halfway to Sunday, you ask that sort of favor." I hadn't thought of asking anybody. So now I was a floor polisher.

The Cross of Lorraine tells the tragic story of the capitulation of the French army, narrated through the nerve-racking confusion, despondency, and anxieties of a small group of agents provocateurs who, against their better judgment, surrender and are transported to a German prison camp. There they realize the poisonous intent of the Nazis, and though one cowardly weakling defects, dignity and self-respect and French nationalist pride finally dictate their heroic actions. It is basically a War Office propaganda film. The Cross of Lorraine itself was originally a symbol of Joan of Arc and was added to the French flag by Charles de Gaulle, adopted as the symbol of the Free French. The film had a few commendable performances by the likes of Lorre, Hume Cronyn, and Joseph Calleia, and a stymied one by Gene Kelly, owing to the stilted script. Much of the story is clichéd. The French Resistance (no mention is made of the Vichy regime) is composed only of the noblest of brave souls; the Germans—with the qualified exception of the Peter Lorre character—are robotic sadists. As for Isador, Lorre had arranged for him a minuscule role as a Nazi prison guard.

So in 1942, Isador, making his first plane flight, traveled to Los Angeles, where he stayed in a cheap hotel and had a total of three days on set. On one of those days, he told me, he got to watch Tommy Dorsey and his band rehearse a scene for *Girl Crazy* on the studio lot. And the day Isador left by cross-country train for home, then senator Harry Truman visited the set, escorted by the head of Metro-Goldwyn-Mayer, Louis B. Mayer. "I was sorry to have missed those big shots," Isador said. "But I'd bet Lazzy said a thing or two to Mr. Truman about the Nazis. I bet he took

Mr. Truman aside and gave him what for. I got to spend a total of about ten minutes alone with Lazzy. Enough for a cigarette. Though he greeted me warmly and introduced me around. In the commissary I sat with other actors playing Nazis. Not that any of this hurt my feelings exactly, and besides, Lazzy was a very busy man. Maybe I shouldn't have gone out there. But I was paid all right, and I believe that Lazzy contributed something extra out of his own pocket. I never set eyes on Gene Kelly. It all was an experience to write in my diary, if I kept one, which I didn't."

Emotionally, as they say, I was in a bad place. Spiritually lost. However, being in Mathilde's old apartment seemed to help, primarily because I'd taken out a book from the library on séances, which contained a chapter on how to conduct them. Using this chapter as a guide, I held one-person séances at the kitchen table. I'd place various of Mathilde's paintings and drawings nearby; I'd prop her final postcard against the candleholder. Mementos and conveyances, talismans and channeling objects. I quickly became a charlatan, a purveyor of false encouragement toward my own self. Passersby looking in through the street-level window would've seen a young man sitting at a table with a freshly ironed tablecloth on it, a single candle in a solid iron holder, and the book on séances open like the Bible, for easy reference.

"Don't tell any of your colleagues at the hospital what you do with this nonsense," Isador warned me. "You tell them, they'll put you in a straitjacket and out come the syringes." He was only half joking. "That typewriter I gave you," he said. "Start writing something. How about you write me a long letter every day. Sit down when you come home from work and type. Anything. I'll provide the envelopes and stamps. Get your imagination up and running."

Isador had far more faith in the rejuvenating, or at least distracting, powers of writing than I knew to have. I continued the séances for weeks. In all that time I thought I heard Mathilde's voice just once, though I suspect I'd fallen asleep at the table and dreamed it, then started awake, confused. "Did you know that [garbled name] used to mix ashes in with his paint sometimes?"—that was the one sentence that flew in from my version of Mathilde's afterlife, as if that dream had been the whole of her afterlife. I suppose this related to Mathilde's having been burned to ash in the airplane wreckage.

Self-generated, idiosyncratic forms of mourning—if that's what I was doing—while excessively indulgent, probably don't harm anyone else, and can for a time sustain a person. They did sustain me at least. My theory was, the best way to prove the depth of my love for Mathilde—the very capacity to love—was never to give in to convenient notions of closure. Do anything to keep the wound open, not merely in order to feel pain, but to feel pain as a way of staying connected.

To that end, I opted for obsessive scholarship about the Saskatchewan landscape. In a way, I suppose I saw that western province as being her cemetery. Before the Internet, researches in the world of antiquarian books and esoteric texts required, to say the least, more fortitude and brainstorming. I'd befriended a professional researcher, Anne Handle, who offered me all sorts of advice on how to obtain monographs, books, and articles about Saskatchewan. I read them one after the other with various levels of comprehension (some were impenetrably "scientific"); this was the closest thing I had, short of setting up house there, to being on the very earth of Saskatchewan.

I should have understood better at the time that the depth of my obsessive dedication to Mathilde after her plane crashed was severely disproportionate to the emotional distance I'd kept from her when she was alive. I never could bring myself to say I loved her. "You don't need to say the words," she said more than once, as if taking jurisdiction over my inability to say them. It wasn't my age, or our age difference; a lot of twenty-year-olds were capable of saying those words and meaning them; it was my fear. One insomniac night I thought, If I say the words I'll have to admit to myself the fact that I mean them. I should have told the truth and said them to Mathilde.

Isador said, "My opinion is, if you move permanently to Saskatchewan, you'd be going overboard. That would be *meshuggeh*. It wasn't your place, it was hers."

My janitorial duties at the hospital went swimmingly. I was never late for work, not once, and Mr. McKenzie took note of that. I got a small raise within two weeks. The hallway of the children's ward was a difficult place to work, because I saw kids who were dealt such bad hands. There was one little girl, Ellen, age eleven. As for her medical condition, all I was privy to was the fact that she suffered seizures. I witnessed one of these, just one, but that was quite enough for permanent memory. Ellen's mother, Jean, often spent the night in the room. Jean was wealthy; her family had a house in the south of France and an apartment in London. Ellen's father was a diplomat of some sort; I saw him only once. But the money was from Jean's family. "They're in import-export," she said.

One time in the all-night hospital cafeteria, Jean said, "You want to know something? Ellen thinks that floor polisher is the funniest thing she's ever seen. She doesn't think you're very good at it. You're not very good at it, are you? But when Ellen sees you push by her door with that unwieldy machine, she just cracks right up. It's like a cartoon to her. You didn't know that, did you?"

"I had no idea. Why's she think it's so funny?"

"Because she does. It's just her sense of humor."

We continued talking, and Jean asked how I'd come to be employed as a night janitor. She seemed truly interested, so I told her how I'd gotten "caught up" at the auction. I remember her saying, "It's like a crime of passion," an analogy I didn't fully comprehend, though it was said with sympathy. She asked more about my life. But I didn't mention Mathilde at all; it seemed too complicated. Too many frayed threads. Over the weeks I spoke with Jean half a dozen more times in the cafeteria. I sat and talked with Ellen a few times, too, and once, during a break, read her twenty or so pages of *A Tale of Two Cities,* which her mother had been reading to her before needing to run home for some reason or other.

In the meantime, I was paying my debt to the auction house. And during the afternoons I was reading about Saskatchewan. I was doing little else, except writing to travel editors and Sunday magazine editors of newspapers throughout Canada and the United States with proposals for writing about birds in places as far-flung and alien to me as Indonesia, South Africa, and Japan—and of course every province of Canada. In each envelope I enclosed my one published article about the birds near Port Medway. My mailbox was not even filling up with rejections, let alone offers of work.

The novels I was reading at the time deftly orchestrated implausibilities along a clear narrative line, but I could not locate such a line in my own life. Every day seemed autonomously haphazard; one day was disconnected from the next. There was no unifying element of thought or strategy, just a bridging ennui and puzzlement. I'd set aside plans to take courses at McGill University. Then, early in March 1970, as she was leaving her daughter's hospital room, Jean offered me a job at her travel agency. I thought it made no sense whatsoever, except perhaps that she felt sorry for me, a wannabe writer pushing a floor polisher around. I wrote travel brochures for her. They had mandatory categories: climate, entertainment, transportation, language—politics was to be avoided. And I was to incorporate upbeat quotes from people who had used Jean's travel agency and had had wonderful times in Egypt, Spain, France, Belgium, Holland, Japan, Brazil, and so on. As for foreign countries, I myself had been only to Canada.

Now I had two jobs and was more confident of paying off my debt to the auction house, but I was sleeping only a few hours a night. Plus, I was often wired on caffeine. I drank up to ten cups of regular coffee a day and, most often in Mathilde's and my old café, at least three espressos. (It was one of the few places where espressos were served in those days.) Sleep usually consisted of catnaps on a sofa in the lobby of the Lord Nelson Hotel. I felt I had more than one address. And in and around all of this, I was still maniacally studying up on Saskatchewan, where Mathilde's ghost might be wandering. My private séances were failing; she wasn't to appear in her old Halifax apartment.

Some days, when Isador was out visiting one of his old cronies from the hotel world or at a movie matinee, I'd work on a brochure at his kitchen table. In late March or early April, I was organizing notes for a brochure about Germany and fell asleep with my head down on the table. When I woke, Isador was watching television and it was nearly time for me to begin my shift at the hospital, so I quickly gathered up my papers and rushed out, scarcely saying goodbye, a little irritated that Isador hadn't woken me earlier, since he knew my work schedule quite well. Anyway, it wasn't until I returned to my apartment the next morning that I examined the notes I'd taken and saw Isador's contribution. Vertically in the margins and between my written lines in a loose-leaf notebook, Isador had provided additions, emendations, and, in bold capital letters, queries such as WHY HAVE YOU NOT MENTIONED WHAT HAPPENED AT TRE-BLINKA AND AUSCHWITZ? Among my notes for transporta-tion: YES THE TRAINS ALWAYS RUN ON TIME IN GER-MANY. Alongside my notes for climate: GERMAN WINTERS ARE COLD AS HELL — DON'T LIE TO INNOCENT TRAV-ELERS! I never spoke to Isador about this.

Jean got a windfall in that an airline became a very lucrative client. And one afternoon, after she had given my brochure on Spain her final approval, she said, "I paid off your debt to the auc-tion house and hope you'll come to work for me full-time. I can find more things for you to do than write brochures. Besides, the brochures are mostly written for this season."

"That is the kindest thing I ever heard, but—"

"Look, you're a mess. Everybody can use some help now and then. You're not so special."

"No, I know that. I just wish you hadn't paid off my debt, Jean. I can't let you. Now I'm indebted to you. Just take it out of my paycheck."

"It wasn't a bribe. Just say thank you. And I'm giving you a small bonus for all your good writing. I only had to change a comma here and there, and maybe take out some adjectives. I've already received compliments on the Holland brochure, you should know. I've been approached by a publisher about a full-blown travel guide. Would that interest you to work on with me?"

"I haven't been anywhere."

"Look, you could start with the pages about Halifax. You could start there."

"I never thought of that."

"See how well we're already working together?"

The guidebook never materialized. Though I did take on more hours and a variety of new tasks at the travel agency, for some reason I didn't give up my janitorial work. Ellen had gotten well enough to leave the hospital, and Jean was spending more and more time away from the office. There was another employee, Bettina, who was about forty but referred to herself as "a local girl." She had indeed been born and raised in Halifax. Bettina ran the day-to-day operation. She went to lunch with prospective clients and fielded telephone calls. I had no deep interest in the travel business, but it was work and I was grateful for it.

One evening at dinner, Isador said, "Even if your Mathilde showed up every time, those goddamn séances don't make for much of a social life." I think he wanted me to appreciate his little joke. "Aren't there any attractive nurses you could go to the movies with or something? You mope around and sleep in the lobby. This is not healthy."

I had no argument there. My social life consisted mostly of dinners with my uncle at the hotel, and with Jean at her house on Sundays. Sometimes Jean and her "paramour," Gus, went out to the movies and I'd watch TV with Ellen, who would regale me with observations about the nurses and doctors she'd known those months she had spent in the hospital. She spared no one her harsh and witty judgments. It cracked me up when she said, "Sorry, sometimes I use adult language." She also admitted to stealing lipstick from the pocketbook of one of the night nurses.

She had a tutor, Grace Eversall, whom Jean hired to get Ellen up to speed in math and social studies, as Ellen had missed so much school. Jean blatantly suggested that if I didn't already, then I should have designs on Grace, who was a student at Dalhousie University. "She told me she's interested," Jean said.

The next Sunday we were together with Ellen, and while Jean prepared dinner in the kitchen, I looked more closely at Grace and let it register how beautiful she was. When Ellen dozed off on the couch after a game of checkers, Grace asked where I lived. But I was so reliant on the belligerent, and to a great extent fraudulent, contingencies of mourning, where I could just as easily have provided Grace with a simple street address, I responded with cruel obtuseness, going into too graphic detail of my relationship with Mathilde, such as it was, or how I wanted to selectively remember it. Grace calmly listened, cool and collected, then said, "I'm so sorry she died. That's really sad. But you know what? I think I once saw you two together. She had on a very cool leather jacket. At first I envied that you were so unusual a couple, you know? I mean, she was so exotic-looking. Honestly, my girlfriends and I wondered what she was doing with you. But after a while I noticed neither of you looked very happy. I'm pretty sure it was you two. You used to hang out at the café right near Dalhousie, right?"

Late one afternoon, I was visiting Isador in his hotel room. He said, "Saturday, do you want to take a drive with me up to Truro? We could spend the night. I'll pay for everything."

"Izzy, what's in Truro that could possibly interest you? You don't even like sitting in a car. And you'd miss your regular Saturday-night chess with the retired bellman. I don't get it."

He fumbled around, rearranging items in his small refrigerator, then said, "I just thought it'd be good to get out of Halifax for a night."

"You look like a kid caught with his hand in the candy jar."

"I never liked candy."

"Well, I'm not going to Truro. The place sounds dull as dishwater."

"Where will you be, then? Saturday."

This dance went on in fits and starts all through dinner. Finally I said, "What's all this about Saturday night, Izzy?"

"There's another auction in the hotel."

"I get it. You're being protective of me. You think if I drop by to watch you playing chess, I'll see the auction and make the same mistake all over again."

"That sort of thing has been known to happen."

"I'll stay a million miles away. What's being auctioned?"

"I only noticed some bird pictures again. Drawings. Paintings. Like last time. Maybe more of a hodgepodge than last time. I don't poke my nose into the auction business. But since it's in the hotel here, I'm apprised."

"I took somebody's Saturday shift at the hospital."

"I understand."

"Okay, then. Are you having any dessert?"

The auction began at eight-fifteen on the dot. There had been a small reception beforehand, which attracted a crowd of about fifty people. I had called in sick to work. I hoped that Mr. McKenzie didn't stop by for a drink at the hotel or come in for dinner with his family. Probably nothing to worry about there. I sat in the back row. After the usual introductory rules and niceties, the first item was put on the block: a rare print called *Black-tailed Gannet,* which Edward Lear had drawn for John Gould's

Birds of Europe. Reading from a note card, a different auctioneer than last time said, "To inaugurate today's proceedings, we have *Black-tailed Gannet,* until recently in private hands. We will accept bids starting at fifteen hundred dollars."

There must be a phrase in the vernacular of obsession to define my actions. *Repetition compulsion* might come close—there certainly was repetition; there certainly was compulsion. But let me put it this way: the winning bid was $2,250, and had there been the same auctioneer as last time, I might have been recognized and tossed out of the room. The difference this time was, thanks to Jean paying off my debt, I had enough in savings to take *Black-tailed Gannet* home to my apartment. Now I owned *Laughing Gull* and *Black-tailed Gannet.*

By April I had decided to take classes at McGill in September, and I told Isador, who said, "Let's celebrate the fact that you've made any sort of decision." That seemed fair. So the next day, a Sunday, we had dinner at the hotel. Afterward we went to his room to have coffee and listen to his favorite radio shows, originally broadcast during World War Two. Many of these shows—gumshoe dramas, westerns, and domestic comedies—still included requests for listeners to buy war bonds, which lent them an air of historical authenticity. The thing was, each time we'd listen to these programs Isador would become despondent. But this particular Sunday his despondency seemed, I don't know, precarious. He seemed drawn darkly down into it. He even started to mumble. I knew that the same old merciless interior harangue had started: *How could I have done it? How could I have acted in that movie? How could I have done it?* Isador appeared to drift away, and I said, "Izzy, maybe you shouldn't listen to these programs anymore."

He snapped, "What the goddamn hell kind of nonsense is that?"

"Well, you become so morbid."

"I'm not having a nervous collapse in front of you, if that's what you're worried about."

"You might have one in private."

"These radio shows bring up all sorts of regrets. That's all."

"That's what I mean."

"I cling to my regrets, once I discover which ones won't go away. I rely on them for unhappiness. It keeps me connected to the past. You're so thick in the skull, you haven't learned anything."

"You like getting so down and out? I don't understand."

"I heard a rumor once that some people don't have any regrets. Now, what kind of person would that be? Do you want to be friends with someone like that? Would you trust someone like that?"

Isador was debating at a depth of philosophical paradox I could not compete with. It had a comical aspect, just the way he said what he'd said, characteristically Isador's way of putting things. I loved him, so I loved his comic-tragic way of inverting logic in order to define himself by his worst moments. I knew that when this whole thing about *The Cross of Lorraine* got most deeply to him, he'd put his scratchy records of Bach's suites for unaccompanied cello and Chopin's nocturnes on the turntable, to accompany and intensify his mood, a duet between sad and sad; and having found a successful way to comport himself at such moments, he stuck with it. Not a few times, when I heard one of these records through his door, I turned around in the hallway and walked back to the electric lift.

Now turning down the radio volume, he said, "Look at my

life. What have I got? My wife's been gone for years now. My children live far away. You're about to abandon me for university. Which is fine. Which is good. A very good thing. Let's just leave it at that, all right? It's hard for you to understand because you didn't live through the war. People who lived through it, they'd understand my unconditional unforgiveness toward myself for taking that part. And Laszlo meant well, I know that. But it's been a curse."

"Isador, there've been hundreds of movies with Nazis in them. Besides, you told me yourself, *The Cross of Lorraine* was a flop. Hardly anyone saw it."

This seemed only to more firmly establish his point of view. "I see it every night—in *here*," he said, putting his finger to the side of his head as if pointing a revolver. "I am not a good man."

"You're a very good man."

"On that subject we differ in our opinions."

We listened to three more hours of radio shows. *The Aldrich Family, Dick Tracy, The Timid Soul, Sherlock Holmes,* and *Mr. Keen, Tracer of Lost Persons.* Isador's absolute favorite was *You Can't Do Business with Hitler,* featuring John Flynn and Virginia Moore, produced by the radio section of the Office of War Information.

In June, sponsored by five separate newspaper commissions (none knew about the others) to write about birds in Saskatchewan, I sat at the kitchen table and mapped out my summer. The cumulative payments would just about cover expenses. I was surrounded by boxes of clothing and books I'd packed up for storage. I'd hung *Black-tailed Gannet* and *Laughing Gull* on a wall in Isador's hallway. I was letting go of the apartment; it was now rented out to a seamstress.

Traveling light (clothes, notebooks, pens, a copy of *The Car-*

rier of Ladders by W. S. Merwin, a field guide to Canadian birds, field glasses, plus that postcard of the couple eloping), on June 5 I flew from Halifax to Regina. From Regina I boarded a small plane to Kyle, just north of Saskatchewan Landing Provincial Park, a few miles from where Mathilde's plane went down. With no professional therapeutic guidelines, but fiercely cajoled by Isador, I knew that if I was going to "move ahead with life" (Isador's words)—detach from séances, detach from the delusion that in time Mathilde would have considered me the love of her life—then I'd best start with an actual location on the map, so I chose the site of Mathilde's death.

It was to be far less a pilgrimage than a chance to begin some sort of new journey. Mathilde had gone to her Maker; I needed to look at her photograph to recall her face, since even dreams seldom provided that now. I had a photograph of her at what I considered her most ebullient, bright self, laughing, seated at a wedding banquet, and when I looked at it in the plane, I smiled at her comment about her pronouncedly angular nose: "I cut a swath through the day." Also, I remembered really liking the dress she had on that evening. The earrings, too. How she was inebriated, giddy, whispering to the woman who sat next to her. And how she'd danced every dance with someone, including me in my rented tuxedo. I'd turned twenty-one in March. Her twenty-seventh birthday would have been June 7.

To get to the site of the wreckage was simple. At the landing strip in Kyle there was a car and a pickup truck for rent by the day or the week. I chose the truck and put twenty dollars in the hands of the attendant. That was commerce in those days. On a road southeast out of Kyle, I found the six-cottage motel where Mathilde had been staying and asked the owner, "Can you please direct me to where the plane crashed last year?" He drew a rough map on a napkin. No questions asked except, "Will you be needing a room?" It took me less than fifteen minutes to get to the spot he'd marked with an X.

It was a beautiful day. There were some birds, but I didn't bother to identify which kinds, since I just wanted to take in the sweep of the landscape. Open fields along a creek, with cattails waving and slightly bent in the wind. As I started to walk, with no destination in mind, I suddenly saw that someone had put up a wooden cross, decorated with plastic flowers, near a small marsh. This had to be in memory of the pilot, or Mathilde, or perhaps both. There were no words on the cross, but it was built solidly and seemed to be planted deep in the ground.

It occurred to me that I should find out who had done this, but then I thought that would make for detective work, the result of which would have little meaning. I wasn't there to write about Mathilde's fate, I was there to write about birds, and that was that. The wreckage had been mostly cleared, but not completely. I noticed a charred seat with its springs exposed, sections of a wing, blackened pieces of glass, and what looked like photographic film cases lying about. There also was part of the fuselage with decaled numbers on it, but I didn't care to touch any of this. I just needed a place to begin.

I ended up staying at the small motel that night. It was only me and the proprietor and his wife; we had hamburgers together in their cottage. Nice people, all seasoned hospitality and grateful for the patronage (twelve dollars for the room), but they thought I wanted to talk about the plane crash, and I may have been snappish and blunt in saying that I didn't. Later, we watched a half-hour sitcom on TV. Having slept fitfully with the bedside lamp on, I left at five a.m. to drive back to Kyle.

From Kyle, in harrowing crosswinds, I flew with three others to Last Mountain Lake, beginning the second day of what would be an exhaustive, two-month tour of Saskatchewan's bird preserves, during which I worked myself to a near frazzle, sleeping at most three or four hours a night. I took detailed notes and snapshots with a Polaroid Instamatic, pictures hardly professional enough for publication, meant only to later help me distinguish, along with my journal, one preserve from the next. In my inexperience, I didn't know how to go about these commissions, except to chronicle everything I could. When I got home, I would figure out how to tailor my pieces to satisfy each editor. In the end, I succeeded in getting only one published.

But along the way, something unforeseen occurred. I began keeping a "life list" of birds, a process that I later came to see as distasteful, reducing the natural world to a kind of arithmetic. Yet during those summer months, keeping a ledger of bird names, each one like a found poem, allowed me some purchase on quotidian life.

I'd wanted to begin with Last Mountain Lake because it was the first designated bird sanctuary in North America. In autumn, a visitor could see as many as fifty thousand sandhill cranes there. Still, it being early summer, I saw peregrine falcons, piping plovers, burrowing owls, ferruginous hawks, loggerhead shrikes, terns, grebes, and pelicans.

After Last Mountain Lake I traveled to the "hummingbird capital," the St. Walburg area; the Battlefords, especially to see the black-crowned night herons; Lloydminster for the yellow-headed blackbirds; Saskatchewan Landing for the belted kingfishers and Clark's grebes; Quill Lake for the red-necked phalaropes and American avocets; Swift Current for the merlins and American kestrels; Grasslands National Park for the greater sage-grouses, prairie falcons, and golden eagles; Weyburn for the chestnut-collared longspurs; Moose Mountain Provincial Park for the great crested flycatchers and ring-necked ducks; Leader (where, sitting near the Leader Bridge, I got bitten on the hand by a prairie rattlesnake and was administered antivenom at the Park Service clinic, and became only mildly nauseous, though my fever spiked to 103 for a few hours; my hand was puffy, achy, and black-and-blue for a week) for the willow flycatchers, long-billed curlews, and violet-green swallows; Chaplin Lake for the thousands of Baird's sandpipers, and the black-necked stilts and tundra swans; Duck Mountain Provincial Park for the barred owls and rare golden-winged warblers; Good Spirit Lake Provincial Park for the pileated woodpeckers; Douglas Provincial Park for the veeries, Cooper's hawks, and migrant thrushes; Gardiner Dam and Danielson Provincial Park for the great horned owls, hairy woodpeckers, and gyrfalcons; Pelican Lake for the American white pelicans; Buffalo Pound Provincial Park for the LeConte's sparrows and Say's phoebes; and finally the long journey north to Wood Buffalo National Park to see—mostly to hear—the whooping cranes.

All summer, while my mind filled with birds trying to push out every other thought, discussions with park rangers and ornithologists, the Cree Indian woman who'd referred to the lifting of cranes from the water as "God-flight," and the thousand traveled miles, I kept thinking of Mathilde ("She would've loved to have seen all this"), though perhaps less and less as the days went on. What helped was the practical philosophy of Robert Frost, from his poem "A Servant to Servants": "the best way out is always through."

In my case, I was working my way through an entire province of birds in order to emerge into whatever came next, and pretty much succeeded. Yet on my last evening at Wood Buffalo Park, I was out by a marsh, the light hazy, the full moon pale under clouds, as if borrowed for the night from a Japanese scroll, when a boisterous flock of about two dozen geese, not in the customary V shape but a more ragged formation, approached the marsh. Painted by the light of that particular dusk, they looked like grey geese descending.

I HATE TO LEAVE THIS
BEAUTIFUL PLACE

~~~

I OFTEN THINK BACK to my Grand Rapids summer of 1964, that confusing time when, as a means of escape, I obsessively studied three or four photograph-filled books on the Arctic region of Canada—its polar bears and foxes, its seabirds and narwhals, its Eskimo (before the word *Inuit* was in proper use) people living in those vast reaches. Had the few months in the bookmobile launched me on a trajectory that led to the Canadian Arctic? Such connections are all but impossible to assume, of course. Life does not travel from point A to point B. A whole world of impudent detours, unbridled perplexities, degrading sorrows, and exacting joys can befall a person in a single season, not to mention a lifetime. First at McGill University, and then at Western Michigan University, I took, sometimes one per semester, courses in various subjects—philology, zoology, literature—finally earning a degree from the Folklore Institute at Indiana University. And I had to keep finding ways to pay tuition. With assistance from professors and museum directors, and a willingness to live in remote places, I signed up for postings in half a dozen Arctic locales in order to record Inuit life histories, medical histories, and folktales. Looking back, I suppose I had some vague notion of writing about all of this, but mainly I needed the money. And these were the kinds of jobs few people volunteered for. To reduce it to practical terms, it was ready work, where and when I needed it. In the end, I think it's fair to say that nearly a decade of piecemeal Arctic jobs and traveling provided an apprenticeship in writing and thinking. The ubiquitous blessing was that I got to experience the languages, cultures, and spirit presences that verified the assertion set forth in a poem by Paul Éluard: "There is another world but it is in this one."

In December 1980, I was in Eskimo Point, in the Canadian Northwest Territories. On the eighth of that month, I wrote on a page of my journal, "Today John Lennon died." That afternoon, in the Arctic's crepuscular light, the Inuit pilot Edward Shaimaiyuk stood next to his Cessna on the hard-packed snow landing strip, which had been sprinkled with crushed coal for traction, and said, "I'm going south to Canada."

Edward was about sixty years old. Leaning against his plane, he began to shout what to my ears were desperate-sounding implorations in his language, the Quagmiriut dialect spoken along Hudson Bay. It had begun to snow hard, and the snow was mixed with slanting sleet. The sky was shifting dark clouds west to east. Edward was addressing Sedna—I distinctly heard the name—who is the ancient and powerful woman-spirit who controls the sea and to some extent the air and ice over the sea. For centuries, ever since she was betrayed by her cousins and exiled to the sea bottom, she has maintained an entourage of sea spirits who do her retributive bidding, and has comported herself with severe and unpredictable moodiness, exhibiting an uncanny repertoire of punishments, some lethal, in response to the cruelty, greed, and spiritual trespasses of human beings. To say that Sedna can act in a capricious manner is to say that there are stars in the sky.

One consequence of Sedna's behavior is that Inuit people have a provisional relationship with her, and must constantly be vigilant not to offend. Sedna has to be appeased daily, and prayer is one way to do this. Prayers as in what Edward Shaimaiyuk was shouting — he knew she was causing weather hazardous to fly in. He was apologizing, seeking forgiveness, although I didn't know for what, exactly.

In its intensity Edward's wild prayer was both mesmerizing and disturbing. He had worked himself nearly to tears. Again, I didn't know for which trespass he was asking pardon — with humankind there were so many and they occurred so frequently — nor did I know if I should even have been looking at him. What is the proper decorum in the presence of such a dramatic and intimate petition for mercy from invisible forces?

Meanwhile, I helped his son, Peter Shaimaiyuk, load five electric guitars and several sacks of mail into the cargo hold. The guitars were going to Winnipeg for repair.

Yet something was very wrong here. Something was not going well. Edward was now staring at the horizon. Studying it. Looking over now and then, Peter, in turn, studied his father's expression.

Though he'd calmed down a little, Edward kept repeating a phrase in Inuit, and finally I asked Peter what it meant.

"It's my father's biggest fear," he said. "His biggest worry. And it's the reason he's not going anywhere today. He's not going to fly, I'm sure of it."

"Would he mind if I knew why?"

"It's hard to put in English," Peter said. "But my father believes that radio airwaves—not sure what word to use. Radio waves—frequencies—from the cities can catch his plane and pull him in like a fishing net. Sedna can cause this. And he's very afraid of this. He doesn't want to be pulled down to a city like Winnipeg or Montreal. He's seen cities in magazines and doesn't want to go there. He doesn't want to go where rooms are stacked up on each other, like in a hotel. He doesn't even like it that rooms are stacked up on each other in the Churchill Hotel, just down to Churchill. He goes to Churchill a lot. He's had bad dreams about having to sleep high up off the ground."

"He flies up in the air, though," I said, as if reason could abide.

"Not the same thing to him. You won't figure it out. Just take it as fact. It's how my father thinks when Sedna gets angry—she's angry today. He thinks she'll make radios from the cities net him and drag him off course. He'll have to land in a city and he'll never get out. He'll die in a city. He doesn't have a lot of fears, my father. But the ones he has, they're big. That's why he's so upset now. That's why he's definitely not flying today. When he gets like this I just step back. He's my father. I've seen this a lot of times. One thing's for sure, my father is not flying. Let's get the guitars off, okay?"

For some fifteen years Peter had a band called Nanook the Gook. The band's name originally was Turbulence (I wonder if it came from his father's experience flying mail planes or from some inner turmoil Peter himself felt), but they decided to change it when the Vietnam War was at full nightmarish cacophony and *gook* was the derogatory term used by the U.S. military for a Vietnamese person; this was the Inuit band's satirical identification with, as Peter put it, "small brown folks." (Nanook was the Inuit fellow who had been featured in the famous ethnographic film *Nanook of the North.*) The Vietnam War came to be referred to as the first television war, but in the Arctic it arrived almost exclusively by radio, via daily bulletins on the CBC.

Anyway, I'd heard Nanook the Gook play four or five times and knew that their repertoire consisted entirely of the songs of John Lennon. Peter, who was about thirty-five, wore round wire-rimmed glasses when he played guitar and sang—no corrective lenses, just clear glass. He had ordered them after he'd heard a commercial for "John Lennon granny glasses" on the radio or seen an ad in some magazine or other. I think maybe it was in *Rolling Stone,* back issues of which were delivered by mail plane every three or four months, depending on the weather.

Though the band itself would most likely never be written up in *Rolling Stone,* Nanook the Gook was for a time enormously popular throughout the scattered villages along the east and west coasts of Hudson Bay and inland. Edward had often flown the band to gigs. I still have a number of reel-to-reel recordings of covers of "Instant Karma," "Power to the People," "Woman Is the Nigger of the World," "Whatever Gets You Through the Night," "Nobody Told Me," "Don't Worry, Kyoko," and "Working Class Hero." The band was heavy on guitars. When I was living in Eskimo Point they had recently taken on a new lead guitarist, who was seventeen. In the recording I have of "Nobody Told Me" you can hear seagulls in the background.

I had been employed by the Arctic Oral History Project for a third year to translate life histories and folktales. In Eskimo Point I was in the midst of transcribing and translating a single, quite complicated story, and the working title I gave it was "I Hate to Leave This Beautiful Place." In broad outline, the story concerns a man who is turned into a goose by a malevolent shaman, and when it comes time for all the geese to fly south, he despairs about leaving; in fact, he falls into unmitigated grief, primarily expressed through a high-pitched wailing lament: "I hate to leave this beautiful place! I hate to leave this beautiful place!" which can be heard at great distances, echoing across the stark tundra. The man who was transformed into a goose was formerly a strong and decent fellow with a wife and two children. He was a great artist whose soapstone sculptures of animals were widely admired. He was reputed to have rarely left the village of his birth, Padlei.

In his incarnation as a goose, the man realizes that unless he migrates with the other geese he will die. His despair at this fate intensifies the story's universal themes of mortality, longing, home, sanity. And the story contains, with the philosophical generosity characteristic of Inuit spoken literature, and without necessarily spelling it out, a meditation on what the world requires of and imposes on an individual attempting to live a dignified existence, and how that person comes to knowledge of him- or herself through indelible experience.

I hate to leave this beautiful place. I hate to leave this beautiful place.

I heard the story from Lucille Amorak, with whom I met on an almost daily basis for a couple of weeks while I was in Eskimo Point. Long dead now, Lucille was at the time in her seventies. She was a wonderful poet as well as a storyteller; her poems, to my mind, represented the spoken and written word in equal measure; they had a crafted informality. Here is one of my favorites:

> *My aunt held a grudge — she forgot why.*
> *My cousin held a grudge — he forgot why.*
> *My father held a grudge — he forgot why.*
> *Lots of things happened in the village,*

lots of things.
People were born — people died — gulls
were everywhere all the time —
the beach and the big boulders on the beach
stayed put.
My cousin lived in another village
and she held a grudge — she forgot why.
I held a grudge — it was against a seal — because
that seal nabbed a fish right off my line!
I don't hold that grudge anymore
but at least I remember why I once did.
My other uncle held a grudge — he forgot why.
My other aunt held a grudge — it was against me.
One day I walked over to her house and said,
"What's your grudge?" "I forgot," she said.
"It was fun holding it," she said, "then it wasn't
any longer."
We sat down for a meal. My aunt was in
a pretty good mood — she laughed a lot —
I forgot what about.

As Lucille's family had never joined a church, her birth was never recorded, but she told me that her mother had told her she had been born in 1913. Lucille was Peter Shaimaiyuk's grandmother's sister. Lucille and I usually worked together from seven in the morning until noon. We sat at her splintery table in her one-room shack, located just down from the post office flying a Canadian flag. She often kept her teapot on the boil, and each morning she'd hold a piece of seal fat to the open end of a flask, and tip the flask to soak the fat in whiskey. Our work often proceeded haltingly; my skills in the Inuit language considerably lacked refinement, and yet Lucille had "a lot of English," as she put it, which was true. We managed.

Anyway, at about eleven p.m. on December 8 I was reading, perhaps for the hundredth time, Merwin's *Carrier of Ladders* in the stockroom of the Hudson's Bay Company store, where I had a cot and washbowl, and shaved without a mirror, all courtesy of Mr. Albert Bettany, the store's manager since 1955. These were sparse quarters, to be sure. But I also had an electric space heater. It was about minus ten or fifteen degrees outside. Suddenly Peter Shaimaiyuk walked in, no knock on the door. "Hey, hey," he said, "Tommy's gonna be on the radio, eh?"

Tommy Novaqirq was the drummer in Nanook the Gook. I sat up in my cot and switched on the shortwave, which came in loud and clear; turning the dial, I found NWT — Northwest Territories Radio. The weather reporter, who was also a news broadcaster, was named Gabriel Alikatuktuk. He alternated between English and Inuit, with a smattering of French as well. He had a wonderfully quirky manner and sometimes out of nowhere would speak in a pretty good imitation of Humphrey Bogart.

One important feature of Gabriel's show was that his weather report often included recriminations. Let me explain.

Through the labyrinthine Arctic gossip routes — mail plane pilots, for instance, were big contributors — Gabriel received all sorts of information about the behavior of people throughout his listening region. The best equivalent I can think of is the crime report in the daily newspaper that serves the hamlets where I live in Vermont, and which archives the disparate incidents (mostly ludicrously petty crimes, yet some are harrowing) that occur there, such as loud talking on the street in the middle of the night, the abuse of a homeless dog, jaywalking, a mailbox smashed in by drive-by teenagers bored to tears, and so on — the cumulative effect being, *Look how much small-time criminal behavior can be crammed into any given day or night.* This is pretty much the same behavior — stupid, reckless killing of time — one experienced in Arctic villages, generally speaking. The difference was, Gabriel Alikatuktuk, in his weather forecast, would choose a specific perpetrator to indict as having insulted Sedna, pissed her off in some terrible way or other. This was how he would delineate the equation between the offending act and the mythological response. So when Tommy Novaqirq had gotten blackout drunk and taken potshots at a neighbor's sled dogs, all but blinding one dog in its right eye, Gabriel Alikatuktuk got wind of it.

"Now, word got to me," Gabriel announced, "that this dumbass fellow named Tommy Novaqirq the other night shot at a neighbor's dogs, and now Sedna is not happy, my friends, she is *not happy.* And there's a freakin' *outrageous* blizzard moving in on Hudson Bay from the northwest, my friends. It's gonna blow the asshole out of a polar bear. It's gonna wail louder than Hendrix doing the national anthem at Woodstock. It's gonna tear into Inuit territories and have a wild time of it. So thanks a lot, Tommy Novaqirq — and I mean, if you weren't such a fantastic drummer . . ."

"Oh shit, Tommy's famous for a bad reason," Peter said.

We were laughing like crazy. And as we listened to more of this radio riff on the relationship between human misjudgment and a threatening weather system, of the sort we'd heard dozens of times before, suddenly the radio seemed to go dead. Silence. Then Gabriel emitted a sharp, sobbing intake of breath and said, "My friends in the northern world." He stopped again. You could hear him trying to catch his breath. There were some weird sounds in the background, too, as if somebody was breaking a table or chair, a furious ransacking. Then Gabriel said, "My friends, John Lennon was murdered tonight in the city of New York in the USA." There was another long silence. Then: "John Lennon was gunned down. John Lennon is gone."

I imagined this radio message physically manifesting itself as a net floating out into the black sky full of the vastest array of stars visible from Earth.

It took less than half an hour for the band to gather in my room—Tommy, Peter, the new guitarist named Sam Karpik, and William Okpik, a guitarist and keyboardist. They all sat in fold-out slat chairs and plugged their guitars into amplifiers attached by extension cord to an auxiliary generator. Tommy set up his drum kit. Gabriel Alikatuktuk, in his studio, started playing John Lennon song after John Lennon song with no commentary at all. Nanook the Gook jammed along with the radio. And while I did not think to write down all the titles, I do recall that during the first three or four songs played, the words were distinctly accompanied by Tommy's fits of sobbing. Plus, everyone was getting very drunk on whiskey. At one point Tommy said, "I'm such a fuckup," and went off on a berserk drum solo that must have lasted ten or fifteen minutes, all the while screaming, "Sedna—pleeeze, Sedna—pleeeze!"

"You can't be thinking that shooting at those dogs had anything to do with what happened down in New York," I said.

Tommy kicked over the drum set, threw the drumsticks at my face, and walked over and took a halfhearted swing at me, which I easily blocked, and then he sat on the floor. "What the fuck do you know about it," he said.

The long Arctic night continued to unfold, with whiskey, cigarettes, the radio, and very little talking. Every once in a while I'd tune in another long-distance station on the shortwave. The death of John Lennon was being talked about in so many languages it was mindboggling. It was a murder translated everywhere.

If I remember correctly, Gabriel Alikatuktuk was broadcasting from Winnipeg. Some years later, and with no small amount of inquiry by letter, I was able to obtain a copy of Gabriel's playlist of that night. It was typed on a manual typewriter: "Cold Turkey," "I Found Out," "Mother," "Hold On," "Working Class Hero," "God," "Imagine," "Crippled Inside," "Jealous Guy," "It's So Hard," "I Don't Want to Be a Soldier," "Give Me Some Truth," "Oh, My Love," "How Do You Sleep?," "Oh Yoko!," "New York City," "Mind Games," "I'm Sorry," "One Day (at a Time)," "Bring On the Lucie," "Intuition," "Out of the Blue," "Only People," "I Know (I Know)," "You Are Here," "Meat City," "Going Down on Love," "Whatever Gets You Through the Night," "What You Got," "Bless You," "Scared," "No. 9 Dream," "Surprise, Surprise (Sweet Bird of Paradox)," "Steel and Glass," "Beef Jerky," "Nobody Loves You (When You're Down and Out)," and "(Just Like) Starting Over."

Nanook the Gook left the stockroom of the Hudson's Bay Company store at about seven-thirty the following morning. Gone sleepless, by eight I was again working with Lucille Amorak. She had been suffering from pneumonia, which had been diagnosed at the small hospital in Churchill; Edward Shaimaiyuk had flown her there and back. Edward was given antibiotics and told how to administer them to Lucille.

As a result of her condition, Lucille was noticeably short of breath and occasionally wheezy, which infused her renditions of "I Hate to Leave This Beautiful Place," as I had come to refer to it, with a punctuated sense of urgency, sentence by sentence — at least that is how it sounded to me on the tape recordings. When she raised her voice for emphasis, or when she shifted into one character or another, she often had to clear her throat and sometimes stopped to catch her breath. She occasionally had to stop for a nap in the middle of a work session. It got to the point where Lucille simply could not continue, even at severely reduced hours. But it was enough. I was fortunate to have a lot of help with the transcription and translation from her husband and two nieces, who went over the story and the vocabulary lists. Finally, on December 21, we closed up shop.

But that morning of December 9, the world seemed haunted by radio, as the CBC, the BBC, and stations out of Vancouver, Amsterdam, London, Buffalo, and other locales continued to report the aftermath of John Lennon's murder and played his songs. I asked Lucille Amorak if she had ever heard of John Lennon, and she said, "I heard about him from Peter. He played me some songs. He sang me some songs. I asked if this John Lennon would be visiting us, and Peter said no, he wouldn't be."

Before I left Eskimo Point, Peter announced that he needed to get down to New York and stand for a while in Central Park near the Dakota apartment building where John Lennon had been shot, "maybe even find some people to play Lennon songs with." He had never been to a Canadian city before, let alone out of the country. He had gotten hold of a map of New York from the library in Churchill and drawn a circle around Central Park.

The ability of Nanook the Gook to make a living was restricted by the long winters — people in the far north didn't travel much until late spring. Still, the band made a little money, and Peter had previously saved some — "not much, but enough" to sponsor his journey to New York. I did not know the nature of his finances in detail, but he had his mind made up. Peter had asked the rest of the band to go with him, but nobody else had any interest, and this caused a rift. I was scheduled to leave from Churchill on the Muskeg Express to Winnipeg; I knew that weather interfered with the train schedule and was prepared to wait at the Churchill Hotel. I remember hearing Peter say, "Sedna is really pissed off these days, eh?" Anyway, I was willing to sleep high up off the ground in the hotel.

But the day before Edward flew me to the Churchill landing strip — a brief jaunt for him, really — Peter insisted that I walk with him about a quarter mile out of Eskimo Point to a frozen marsh. It was cold as hell and I was fighting off the flu and hadn't thought it too wise to accompany him, but he was carrying his electric guitar and a small amplifier with a battery wrapped in packing material to protect it from the cold, so my curiosity was up. I had no earthly idea what he had in mind and did not ask.

When we reached the marsh, a few ravens flew off and I looked out toward the center of an iced-over open area and saw a snowy owl; it was a big owl and did not move at all, except for a slight flutter of its wings and a subtle head-bobbing, its eyes not blinking but opening and closing with signal mysteriousness. The owl was almost camouflaged by the snow and snow light. Nonetheless, once you saw it, you could glance away and locate it again, because it had not moved an inch.

No words were exchanged between Peter and me. He removed the battery from its wrapping, set the wrapping down on the frozen ground, and put the battery on top. He plugged the guitar into the amp and the amp into the battery. He tuned up and made the guitar whine and echo, and he sang the opening bars of "Whatever Gets You Through the Night," and I mean blasting it out over the tundra. Amid the piercing music the owl shifted only slightly and tucked its head deep into its breast and closed its eyes. This struck me as sad and comical and another of those things I cannot put words to.

". . . through the night, all right, all right." Peter had a voice that made Bob Dylan seem like Pavarotti, but what did it matter? With desperate, joyful abandon he shouted, "I got my Eskimo freak on!"—wildly gyrating in classic rock-star style, wailing. He was torn up inside, is what I thought. And I had never seen, up to then or since, tears actually fly from someone's face. When he finished the song, in an exaggerated way he bowed to the owl and said to me, "I've played for this fellow eight or ten times, you know."

I had heard that for well over a year Gabriel Alikatuktuk blamed the worst Arctic storms on Mark David Chapman, the sick creep who had murdered John Lennon, though he continued his tradition of blaming Inuit people for trespasses and violations, too. (In fact, it was on his radio broadcast that I first heard assertions about air pollution causing climate change, which agitated Sedna almost beyond imagining.) I never saw Peter again, but did learn that he eventually made his way to New York in December of 1981, in time for the first anniversary of John Lennon's death, and got to play Lennon songs with musicians and singers in Central Park across from the Dakota. Edward said that his son had "got all caught up" in the city for the rest of that winter. Early in the summer of 1982, Peter had traveled by bus and apparently for days on foot to Flin Flon, Manitoba, and from there his father flew him back home to Eskimo Point. Edward said that almost immediately upon his son's return, "spirits started using him." I did not understand the full context of that phrase, but I knew it referred to malevolence. The way Edward put it was, "Peter was done in."

Though I once entertained the idea of writing a musician's

biography of Peter, the fact is that for years I had no notion of his situation or his whereabouts, nor did I seek any of it out. I can only claim the slightest knowledge of his life after I saw him play "Whatever Gets You Through the Night" on that bone-chilling bright day outside of Eskimo Point. But when I returned to that village a few years later, one of Peter's cousins suggested that I walk to the old Eskimo cemetery and find Peter's grave. Naturally I did that. On his grave marker, a simple wooden cross, with his name and the years of his birth and death, it read: *Nobody Told Me There'd Be Days Like These.*

I ended up writing a reminiscence based on journals I had kept in the late 1970s when I was working in Churchill, Manitoba, where I met one of the most inimitable personages in my life, a woman named Helen Tanizaki; the book was called *In Fond Remembrance of Me.* Helen introduced me to many of the things that have sustained me since: Japanese literature; an appreciation for uncanny narrative strategies and wildness of incident in Arctic folktales, which affected the emotions in a different way than Western, beginning-middle-end stories did; and the habit of keeping a notebook and journal, which may sound obvious but wasn't to me at the time. And Helen was the first person I had ever known who was tossed and turned by self-inflicted theosophical arguments — a mixture of Buddhism and what she called "handmade" theories of predestination and the afterlife, things like that. She didn't have much longer to live — she had stomach cancer when I knew her — and spoke of her haunted preoccupations with an honesty and directness I had not previously experienced. I don't want to sentimentalize our few months of proximity to each other — she was working in translation, too, at a much higher level than I was capable of, and I tried very hard to tell things straightforwardly in *In Fond Remembrance of Me*. But forty-some years later, her belligerent and graceful sensibility and her spiritual intensity provide a template for what is possible in a life.

You might say that my time in the Arctic was an apprenticeship, for writing and thinking and even for attempting to keep certain aspects of the past as close at hand as humanly possible.

In late spring of 1981, I went to yet another Eskimo village, Pangnirtung, in the Northwest Territories, to record folktales. Suffice it to say that I was pleased to have the employment, given the fact that I still had no career to speak of and was financially at loose ends. My Pangnirtung notebook was titled "Horizon/Fear," because the stories I worked with there were about threatening entities — horrendous spirits, malevolent weather, terrifyingly strange beasts — appearing on the horizon. Simply put, the repertoire of spirit beings seen on the horizon in those folktales was truly prodigious and disturbing.

What was especially breathtaking in these stories were the currents of anxiety, the intensification of panic, and the acceleration of events that were caused by the first sighting of such harrowing spirits.

In one folktale, when a ten-legged polar bear is seen on the horizon, a number of marriages suddenly take place. In another tale, when it is determined that a giant ice worm is navigating toward a village, a number of murders are committed, all in a single night. In yet another, when the horizon roils up dark clouds that speak in ventriloquial echoes — that is, the clouds seem to be speaking from places other than the ones they are occupying — a number of pregnancies are cut short and children are born months before they otherwise naturally would have been. Healthy children born into a world in extremis. In another folktale, a spirit being with arms that look like awls is reported to be traveling toward a village. In hearing this news, most everyone living there falls victim to a kind of radical arrhythmia—not only do people's heartbeats suddenly accelerate and then just as suddenly become alarmingly slow, but hearts literally "toss people about the village" as if a wind were blowing from inside their bodies.

Eventually I translated eight of these "Horizon/Fear" stories, but as it turned out, I left Pangnirtung before my assigned linguistic work was completed—for two reasons.

First—and such an experience is difficult to describe—the stories got to me. Their plots began to take hold of me beyond all my powers of resistance, to the point where I began consciously to avoid looking at the actual horizon—just while walking between houses, for instance. It takes a great deal of willfulness, or fear, to *not* look at the horizon in an Arctic landscape, especially in a place like Pangnirtung, with its harbor containing flotillas of newly formed ice in all their sculpted shapes and sizes, out where dark birds disappear, where the light shifts its tones hourly, where whale geyser-spumes hang in wavering columns of mist for up to ten minutes after the whales pass by, like signatures composed on the air. One probably should not be in a place like Pangnirtung if one does not wish to take in the horizon, is the conclusion I came to. The horizon, where the rest of the beautiful world resides. Avoid that, and you start to go too far into yourself.

The second and far more compelling reason I fled Pangnirtung was that, during what turned out to be my final week there, I experienced a number of exceedingly unpleasant, often physically violent run-ins with an *angakok*—a shaman. The world of Arctic shamans has enough ethnographic complexities to fill volumes; still, it has to be experienced to be believed. This particular fellow did not have a name, at least I never heard him called by one. He was perhaps fifty or fifty-five, stocky, with a face deeply lined both latitudinally and longitudinally, especially in certain precincts of his forehead. He had a gouged, almost grotesquely cauliflowered left ear and dark reddish-brown skin with splotches of lighter brown, each of which seemed to have been outlined in ash. His right eye was filmed over. To put it directly, he cut an alarming figure.

He had a habit—or a scare tactic—of uttering a phrase first in Inuit, then in broken French, then in English, all more or less sotto voce, as if speaking to two other people who resided inside himself. He wore boots with no laces, frayed thick trousers, two shirts under two sweaters, all beneath a parka. He had lots of snowy-owl feathers haphazardly festooning his hair (as if transforming himself from an owl into a human being, or vice versa), which was filthy and matted. He also wore a kind of necklace that consisted of half a dozen small transistor radios tied together with twine. (I remember thinking back to Edward Shaimaiyuk's vigilance concerning the possibility of radio waves netting his plane. I even—and I realize now this thought contained no small measure of myth-based paranoia—wondered whether this *anga-kok* was one of Sedna's lackeys.)

This *angakok* hated me from the get-go; it was impossible not to comprehend this. How did I know? Because when we first encountered each other in front of the village's convenience store, he said, "I hate you." I may well have been a surrogate for every Caucasian who ever set foot in Pangnirtung throughout history, and could fully understand that anger. Still, this was our first exchange.

From the moment he had arrived in Pangnirtung ("from

somewhere out on the horizon," as one of my hosts put it), he took my presence as a portent of severe weather — and possibly of starvation — in the offing. He immediately began to speak of me in this light. He loudly declared his indictments in front of the convenience store, somewhat in the manner of a crazy person on a city street declaring the end of the world. He smoked cigarette after cigarette (he chewed and spit out the butts) and rattled his transistor radios. I was told by more than one citizen of Pangnirtung not to take his actions personally, but how could I not? Such in-your-face assaults cannot be made less frightening by placing them in the context of historical rage — at least I was not capable of that. It was all expert psychodrama and left me shaken to the core.

"This fellow hates anyone who isn't Inuit," an elderly woman told me. "And he hates most Inuit people, too." Hardly a comfort, but at least it clarified things a bit.

Some people advised me to try to ignore him; others suggested that I leave on the next mail plane out. Both made sense. My host family was kind and generous, and provided me a comfortable room to sleep in, but I definitely understood my outsider status — this wasn't new to me. Generally speaking, after this *angakok* arrived, the village went about its daily business, except that this raving maniac was there. On a number of occasions I saw him standing near the counter of the convenience store, windmilling his arms, shouting incomprehensible things (though maybe not incomprehensible to the spirit world) in a language that only in part consisted of Inuit, or even French or English, words.

On other occasions I would see him standing off to one side of the store, smoking a cigarette or a pipe, scrutinizing me. And one time he shouted, "You have to eat food. I eat weather." This strange locution imposed the same kind of arrhythmia on me that I had heard about in one of the "Horizon/Fear" folktales, or at least that's what it felt like. I had to get out of there fast.

I wanted to fulfill the terms of my employment, though, and had to deal with this fellow in some way, so one day I walked up to him and said, "Leave me alone. I'm not here much longer anyway." His response was to turn on every one of the transistor radios, which seemed in good working order, but because we were in Pangnirtung, far out of all but shortwave radio range, all he could produce was static. Therefore his necklace became an orchestra of hisses and scratches. Then he stubbed his cigarette out against the shoulder of my coat.

"There is another world, but it is in this one," wrote Paul Éluard. With this *angakok*, I definitely was in another world. I could hardly claim any deep knowledge of Pangnirtung, but I did know that throughout the Arctic people believed that shamans were capable of causing illnesses, and in turn were paid to demonstrate their ability to cure those illnesses—a perverse strategy that had apparently worked for centuries. I could see that the *angakok* harassing me was indeed respected, or at least feared, for proven reasons; he scared the hell out of me. One other thing I knew was that *angakoks* often had a direct line of communication to the spirit world. In other Arctic communities I had witnessed elderly people paying shamans to petition certain presiding spirits for luck and good health, and to deliver family news to ancestors in the land of the dead.

I tried another scheme. I approached my nemesis, who was smoking his pipe near the convenience store, and offered to pay him to fly to the moon and stay there until my work was done. I was told by three different people that this particular *angakok* was quite capable of flying to the moon.

He jammed his thumbs up into my nostrils and pushed me so hard that I stumbled backwards. This was shockingly painful. I took this to mean that my request had been denied. He said, "You walk backwards well. Why not walk backwards home now." I told him that my home was thousands of miles away. He said, "Start now before the bad weather." Later I was told by a bystander that I had misinterpreted what the *angakok* had muttered. What he actually said was, "Start now before I bring in bad weather."

In Pangnirtung I worked with storytellers in the morning and spent the afternoons transcribing tapes, getting help with vocabulary, filling notebooks, and walking around town and its outskirts. I especially enjoyed visiting the cemetery, where simple white crosses were bowed daily by wind off the sea. Every time I visited late in the afternoon, I saw an elderly woman dressed in winter bundling who would walk from cross to cross, setting them upright again, tapping them down with a hammer.

Though I never asked, I assumed this was her daily task, perhaps self-appointed. What is more, she was the only Inuit person I had seen being accosted by the *angakok*. I observed him walk up to her in the cemetery, mumble something, and push her down. She rose to her feet and spit at him. This struck me as a scenario borne through the ages—it could have happened a hundred years ago, or two hundred, or a hundred years from that afternoon, a timeless confrontation with no discernible reason behind it, though I did not know what personal history there was between the old woman and the *angakok*, nor whether it had anything to do with her association with the Christian cemetery. No matter. This *angakok* was a nasty piece of work. He had arrived at Pangnirtung a menace and built on that daily. I saw this unfold.

In the few Inuit villages I had worked in before Pangnirtung, recording, transcribing, and translating oral literature had given me insight into the mental culture and mythic history of a community, although that is putting things in too academic a light. But in Pangnirtung it didn't work out that way. Every moment in that village seemed off-kilter somehow; I could not get any real purchase on life there. In Pangnirtung, the stories themselves seemed natural forces to be dealt with. They had put my nerves on edge.

Fairly early in the translation process I began to feel that despite an increasing fluency in the language, I was ill equipped to perform my work with any semblance of poise or competency. Still, I was being paid a decent salary and all of this was a unique experience. I wanted to see it through.

But night after night in my dreams I reprised the Inuit narratives. It got to the point where I imposed insomnia on myself, preferring not to sleep in order to avoid that endless loop of stories. This was my situation; I had to look at it directly. Finally a person has to sleep—but I wasn't sleeping, not really. Brief naps here and there, no more than fifteen minutes at a time, for six, seven, eight days running. It was not so much my drinking too much black coffee as it was that the characters in my dreams— the characters in the Inuit folktales—were constantly drinking black coffee.

Strange but true. Sometimes they ate coffee grounds.

Stenciled in outsize black lettering on the side of the convenience store, in both Inuit phonetics and English, were the words *Blessed Be the Cheerful Buyer.* Accompanying the words was the painted figure of Jesus handing some Canadian dollar bills to a merchant. On closer inspection, this Jesus had an uncanny resemblance to the rock-and-roll legend Jim Morrison (perhaps the sign painter was a fan). The store carried all manner of goods and necessities: winter clothing, canned foods, rifles, ammunition, pharmaceutical products. At the back of the store, on a chair next to the coal-burning stove, I often sat and worked on the stories.

One late afternoon, Michael Pootgoik, who was about forty and who managed the store, showed me some snow globes he had just unpacked from a shipment delivered by mail plane, along a route that originated in Winnipeg and serviced many Arctic villages, including Churchill. The pilot's name was François Denny; he had gone into the store to take a nap on a cot in the supply room. "He snores like a walrus," Michael said. "I have to put the radio on."

There were two dozen glass snow globes in the shipment. Each contained a diorama of an indoor or outdoor scene in miniature. As he dusted each globe with a moistened cloth and inspected it for hairline cracks, Michael also turned it upside down and then right side up so that the fabricated snowflakes inside fell like confetti on the interior tableau. There was a Christmastime village, perhaps somewhere in New England, with a Christmas tree in the town square decorated with angels; children sang carols on the porch of a house. There was a hunter wearing a checked flannel shirt, black trousers, snow boots, and a thick fur hat, aiming his rifle at a buck with its head turned upward to the falling snow. There was a line of three hula dancers wearing grass skirts and no blouses, their breasts hidden by extravagant leis (seeing these Hawaiians in the snow made us both laugh). There was Little Red Riding Hood pursued by the Big Bad Wolf. There was—my favorite—a string quartet sitting in individual chairs on a bandstand in the middle of a tree-lined park. There was a blacksmith shaping a piece of iron in his shop, which was shown in cutaway relief, complete with bellows and hammers and tongs. There were ice-fishing shacks on a pond. There was a cluster of stars and planets on the ground, as if fallen from the heavens in their original array. There was a rural schoolhouse with children on its playground. And there were others I cannot recall.

"Most every family in Pangnirtung has one of these," Michael said.

The next day, I decided to purchase a snow globe as my going-away gift in reverse, for Mary, the five-year-old daughter of my host family. The moment I stepped into the convenience store out of the cold slanting rain that was forming black ice on stretches of road, I saw the *angakok* curled up in the fetal position on the floor near a shelf that contained power tools. I hoped that he was asleep.

Michael was working the counter as usual. I told him I wanted to buy a snow globe for Mary and asked to see the inventory. "I already sold four," he said, "but I'll set out the rest." He lined up the globes on the counter. I took my time looking them over. "Which do you think Mary might like best?" I asked.

"Why not bring her in and have her pick one out?" Michael said.

"Except that would ruin the surprise."

"A surprise is over quick and then you still have to hope you made the right choice, eh?"

"Okay. Good idea."

I left the convenience store purposely avoiding the *angakok*. I found Mary, and as she and I walked into the store she pointed at the shaman and said, "That man stinks. I'm not afraid of him. He can hurt me and he stinks but I don't care."

Mary, a chubby little kid with the sweetest face and the brightest, most stalwart disposition on earth, should have been my teacher in all things having to do with that miserable *angakok*. At the counter, she was delighted to be able to pick out a snow globe. "I think you're giving me a present because I put a lot of sugar in tea when I make it for you," she said. She sat on the counter, dangling her legs, and picked up snow globe after snow globe, studying each one with the utmost seriousness. Finally she said, "I want this one." She held up the snow globe with the hula dancers inside.

I paid for the gift and handed it to Mary, who then walked out of the store. The *angakok* shouted something at her and she burst into tears and fled. She dropped the snow globe just outside the store and kept on running. I picked it up and put it in my coat pocket.

Back in the store now, I glared at the *angakok* and he glared right back. "Okay, got to deliver some boxes to the clinic," Michael said. "Be back in a short time." He lifted two boxes and a somewhat larger one, balanced them in his arms, and left by the back door. If I had been in my right mind, I would have followed him. But I just stood there next to the remaining snow globes.

Then I heard the transistor radios. This creeped me out no end.

I turned and saw that the *angakok*, whom I could smell from across the store, was sitting up and leaning against the wall. He was holding a screwdriver with the sharp end right up against an electric wall socket, as if he were about to jam the screwdriver into it. He was madly grinning, many teeth gone, and bobbing his head back and forth as if he alone could detect a lively tune inside the cacophony of radio static. Perhaps most arresting of all, he was holding a teddy bear. The store carried a variety of stuffed animals: owls, bears, tigers, walruses, seals, ravens.

The *angakok* stood, dropped the screwdriver on the floor, walked over to a shelf, and took up a sewing kit. He retreated to his corner, where he removed his mangy overcoat and began to sew the teddy bear to it by its four legs. Then he turned up the volume of each of the transistor radios. When finally he slid to the floor, a number of radio batteries fell from his coat pockets.

I do not know to this day what reckless impulse compelled me to deepen the antagonism between us, except that I wanted something to happen, something to end it once and for all. I walked to the shelf that held the stuffed animals, found an identical teddy bear, looked at the price tag, and said, "Don't forget to pay the nine dollars for that bear." I pointed to the stuffed bear he had sewn to his overcoat.

"You know how I'll pay for this bear?" he said, as if choking on the English words, as if he had rocks in his throat.

"No."

"I will tell Pootgoik I'm not going to put him inside one of those," he said, pointing to the snow globes. "He will give me as many bears as I want."

I did not know how to respond. He said, "But you choose—*you* choose which one you want to live inside. Right now—choose!"

"Keep the fuck away from me!" I said with all the force I could muster.

I walked along the side of the store opposite him and out the front door. Mary was standing not more than twenty yards away; she had been watching the store. I handed her the snow globe with the hula dancers inside. I attempted a little joke: "I wouldn't mind being in there with those hula dancers." Which of course hardly registered at all with Mary, and she did not laugh or even crack a smile; she ran off toward her house.

Then I saw Michael returning empty-handed from the clinic.

He walked up to me and said, "Did he steal anything while I was gone? I know he did. What did he take?"

Humiliated, dispirited, hapless, infantilized—you name it—my catalogue of despondency seemed endless in my interactions with this *angakok*. Maybe this is how it should be, I thought, this is what I deserve, representing as I must centuries of colonial intervention, or something like that, though I was in Pangnirtung only as a kind of stenographer for elderly people who told folktales that I fully understood to be indispensable and sacred to Inuit culture and history.

But this *angakok* couldn't care less what I knew or didn't know, or if I did or did not harbor good intentions. He wanted me to walk backwards two thousand miles south. So far he had followed me from grave marker to grave marker in the cemetery, muttered at me, spat at me, jammed his thumbs up my nostrils, and threatened to imprison me in a snow globe. I had to admire his inventive tenacity even while wanting him to disappear. Even knowing he might kill me. Part of his résumé as an *angakok* was that he had killed people.

He had won. Whatever battle we were having, he had won it. I could already feel myself leaving Pangnirtung. Such a beautiful place, really, but it had become impossible for me. Let's face it, I thought, I have become unhinged. In the convenience store Michael said, "This *angakok* won't leave until you leave."

So I arranged for a flight out. The morning before I left, however, I recorded a story, which when typed out amounted to only a couple of pages. A woman named Jenny Arnateeyk—she was the elderly caretaker of the cemetery—told it, and I gave it the title "The Visitor Put in a Snow Globe," which pretty much sums up the plot.

The Visitor Put in a Snow Globe

A visitor arrived and an angakok arrived at about the same time and things got bad right away. The next day the angakok put the visitor inside a snow globe. He got right to it. He didn't hesitate. Then the angakok dropped the snow globe through the ice.

The snow globe floated up again and could be seen just under the ice if you rubbed the snow away with the side of your hand. A lot of people did this, mostly children.

Some days passed by. The angakok said, "Have you noticed how much better the weather has been since I dropped that snow globe through the ice? Have you noticed how many fish have been caught? How much better everyone is eating these days?"

When children looked at the snow globe, they saw that the visitor was keeping busy. He had a little house in there. He had a fireplace that never ran out of wood, so he kept warm. It didn't seem so bad except he was under the ice. That had to be strange for the visitor. Children visited him every day — that must have been good for him.

One day the angakok said, "I'm going a long way to visit some ravens. Then I'm going even farther to visit some other ravens. When I'm gone, don't take pity on the fellow inside the snow globe. If you let him out, the weather will be terrible and all the fish will swim great distances away."

But when the angakok left to visit the ravens, the people in the village took pity, and they got the snow globe out from under the ice. Then the visitor was his normal size again, and he said, "Thank you. I was only visiting."

"How was it inside a snow globe?" someone asked.

"Unusual."

"Well, then — you'd better leave."

The visitor left on a mail plane. The villagers waited for the weather to turn and for all the fish to leave. But the weather stayed all right, and there were plenty of fish to eat. The villagers hoped the angakok kept visiting ravens for many years to come. All this happened quite recently.

I returned only once to Pangnirtung, to write about soapstone carvings, in late August of 1992, taking the hour-and-a-half flight from Frobisher Bay to the village's airstrip. I stayed with an Inuit host family for a week; their prefabricated house overlooked Pangnirtung Harbor. My hosts assured me that it was "too early" for any *angakok* to arrive, and I was greatly relieved. It was clear that my previous visit had become part of local lore, and from the little I could gather, my difficulties at that time had become a kind of entertainment.

Once I had unpacked, I went to meet the three soapstone carvers whose work I was to write about, and they told me that only weeks earlier a photographer from Nova Scotia had been in the village to take pictures. This turned out to be Robert Frank, one of the great twentieth-century photographers. Frank's five-day visit to Pangnirtung is not a part of his biography much mentioned, but to my mind the photographs he took there — the stark, bouldered terrain, the hardened mud roads, the prefabricated Inuit houses, the graveyard — are commensurate on every level with the photographs he took over the course of decades in various parts of Nova Scotia. In a book titled *Pangnirtung,* he writes: "Prefabricated homes along the main road in Pangnirtung. At times a decorated window—reflections inside or outside. Stones—maybe a balance of sky above . . ."

In the autumn of 2006, I visited Robert Frank in his Bleecker Street apartment in Greenwich Village, a few days before we held an onstage conversation at the New York Public Library. I had brought him an Inuit drawing of a spirit hut composed by an artist in Eskimo Point. We listened to a Bob Dylan album, went to dinner on First Avenue. When we returned to his upstairs workroom, he rummaged around in a filing cabinet until he found a folder labeled "Pangnirtung." He removed three photographs, signed and dated them, and offered them as a gift to me.

I was moved by this spontaneous generosity. I looked at the photographs and mentioned that I recognized a house in one of them, which had a poster of a tiger in the window, a tropical beast in the Arctic, open-mawed with sharp teeth showing. We both recalled Canadian flags displayed in other windows. I said that Pangnirtung was one of the bleakest places I had ever been in, yet the people, with a few exceptions, were quite hospitable. Robert Frank said he remembered seeing the complete weather-bleached skull of a whale in the graveyard. That evening in his apartment, we spoke mainly about Pangnirtung. He had fond memories of the place. He had especially liked the graveyard. "It's beautiful there, don't you think?"

Two days before I left Pangnirtung on my second visit, the band formerly known as Turbulence, formerly known as Nanook the Gook, and now called Night All Day, came to town. Edward Shaimaiyuk had flown them in. The only member of the original group remaining was the drummer, Tommy Novaqirq, whose radio indictment back in 1981 was still vivid in my memory. By my estimate, Tommy was nearly forty years old now—"an aging rocker," he said self-mockingly. He looked more than a little the worse for wear. He was quite surprised to see me, not only because ten years had passed, but what was I doing in Pangnirtung anyway? When we got the niceties out of the way, he said, "Well, yeah, people just kind of run into each other up here, don't they?"

The band traveled light. They set up their minimal equipment—instruments, speakers, and microphones—in a kind of warehouse space. Their performance drew about two dozen people of all ages. There was some makeshift shuffle-dancing, some drunkenness, and a few teenage girls who wanted to travel with the band. "Not too many people in the room," Tommy said later, "but we had the music cranked up loud so everyone in Pangnirtung could hear it, eh?"

At the outset of the performance, the lead singer mentioned that Tommy was the only original member of Nanook the Gook and that they had CDs for sale. Then Night All Day launched into the first of five consecutive John Lennon songs, and I thought, So strange—all these years, the repertoire hasn't changed at all. But after a brief intermission a young Inuit guitarist (I never learned his name) began a medley of stunning vocal imitations of the most popular Canadian artists: Neil Young, Joni Mitchell (his version a little too falsetto, but still splendid), Robbie Robertson, Gordon Lightfoot (performed with notable mockery), and a heart-wrenching rendition of the McGarrigle Sisters' "Heart Like a Wheel." During the second intermission I told the young guitar player that with the exception of Gordon Lightfoot, those were some of my favorite singers. "You being the one European in the room, no big surprise there, eh?" he said, laughing, and I laughed, too. "But me too, I love them singers, but they ain't the only Canadians with talent."

Late in the evening, I sat drinking rotgut coffee with Tommy in a small room adjacent to the post office, just the two of us. His facility with English was much improved since I had first met him. He told me he was still living in Eskimo Point and now took care of his two daughters; his wife had left him for good. He filled me in on the other original members of Nanook the Gook, especially about the fate of Peter Shaimaiyuk and his time in New York City, where he had been arrested and jailed for running out on a hotel bill. There was no particular reason for him to reminisce with me, except the fact that I asked questions and he didn't seem to mind answering them; back in 1981 I had been just another "come-and-gone-type visitor" to the Arctic. He did become more animated when we spoke about the night John Lennon had been murdered. "It was bad for everyone," he said. "Bad for everyone. Still is. Them songs don't get old, though, eh? I feel beat to shit, but the songs don't."

For a while we listened to music and news on the post office's shortwave. "Radio from the cities," he said. He closed his eyes and dozed off in his chair. I sat watching him sleep. His electric guitar — he played both guitar and drums — was propped against the wall, plugged into a small speaker. I thought back ten years, trying to recall what he looked like. And then he nodded off for about an hour — expert, it seemed, at sleeping in chairs. When he woke he pulled out a flask, took a deep pull, and said, "You remember Mrs. Amorak at all? Lucille?"

"Of course I do. I think of her often. I know she died."

"Oh, yeah, that's true. She crossed over into the old Eskimo place, like we say. So did her sister and brothers. Natural causes — nobody fell through the ice or nothing."

He smiled. "Want to see a picture of my daughters?"

We exchanged billfold photographs of our daughters. "Mine

were taken by a cheap camera," he said. His daughters were six and four.

"They're so beautiful," I said. "Lucky they don't look anything like you."

"Yeah, right right right, ha. Their mother's down in Winnipeg. One-way ticket, eh?"

"Sorry to hear that."

"But Lucy Amorak. I put some of her poems into songs, and some parts of the stories she told, you know?"

"I've got all of her poems, Tommy. I read them all the time. I don't talk about it much, but I read them."

"Listen to this." He picked up the guitar, adjusted a few dials, tuned it, and tore into some Eric Clapton–style licks for about a minute, then sang: "I like the wind in my hair, I like the sun on my face, the airplane's waiting on the dirt runway, but I hate to leave this beautiful place." More guitar for a couple of minutes, then the refrain: "This beautiful place, this beautiful place, this beautiful place. I hate to leave this beautiful place."

KINGFISHER DAYS

〜✕〜

IN 1990, THE SECOND FULL summer in our 1850s farm-house in Vermont, everything I loved most happened most every day, with exceptions. For one thing, I ran a fever of between 99.5 and 102 for nearly three months. A doctor in Montpelier said of my condition, "I'm not alarmed. Probably it's a strain of flu. Or a low-grade infection. But tests proved inconclusive. Over-all, though, you're able to function normally, right?" I didn't quite know how to answer. Also of concern that summer, my older brother was on the lam again and telephoning at odd hours, try-ing to get me to smuggle him over the Canadian border. And another thing: our well went dry. And another: a resident king-fisher at a beloved sawmill pond about ten minutes' drive from my house was exhibiting a progressive malaise. This was strangely disturbing. I visited this pond almost daily. On the cover of my journal I'd written "Kingfisher Days." I kept suspecting my fever of imposing a kind of unreality, also radical shifts of mood. I'd purchased three different brands of thermometers, perhaps hop-ing that one would render me fever-free.

According to my journal, it was three p.m. on June 22 when my brother telephoned. I took the call in the kitchen. My wife, Jane, had a diagnosed flu. She was listening to NPR and not in bad humor—it was just very hot outside. Our daughter, Emma, a little over two years old, was taking a nap. She had a slight flu as well. It was difficult to separate the heat and humidity of the air from that of the body. The region was suffering a drought; so far, fifty-nine days without rain. "Look, buddy," my brother said, "I'll ask about other things later. But right now I have an urgent situation. What's that noise I'm hearing?"

"It's been what, about two years since I've heard from you?"

"What's that noise?"

"I'm having a well drilled. I bought a farmhouse here."

"Nice tone you're taking with me. I haven't exactly been getting bulletins of your life. I guessed you were in Vermont. I got your number from information. They give out phone numbers, they don't say whether it's a fucking farmhouse or a fucking *outhouse*, okay? My big-shot brother the landowner with his farmhouse."

"It's not like that. I've got a mortgage."

"Well, let me inform you of something. I don't own a house. But I can go back to my motel room and stick my face under the bathroom faucet, turn the water on for all day if I want to. I can *drown* in it. I don't have to put out money for a well."

"You sound like you're in a better mood than the last time we talked."

"I need you to get me into Canada."

"What do you mean?"

"Last I heard, Vermont still shares a border with Canada. I need to cross it. You'd be at the wheel. You know, we could talk. We could catch up a little."

"You want me to slip you over the border so we can have some quality time together?"

"One could go hand in hand with the other is what I'm saying."

I hung up.

From the farmhouse, you drive down the dirt road past the nineteenth-century schoolhouse, cross the Pekin Brook fire bridge, continue onto Pekin Brook Road, turn left past the Calais town hall, and go straight to the four-corner crossroads, Kent Corners. Turn right onto Robinson Cemetery Road and you will shortly come to the old sawmill and millpond, its waterfalls so loud you have to step ten yards back from it to be heard. The pond is now a nature preserve. It's a modest-size pond, perhaps an eighth of a mile in circumference, and there are trees along the shore and up the surround. For as long as I can remember there have been two resident kingfishers raising families on this pond. It is a peaceful place.

The daughter of friends, Olivia, had come to our house to look after Emma. So, following my brother's telephone call, I was able to drive over and sit by the pond. A light rain brailled the surface; there was early mist between the cattail stalks; changes in water and air temperature often registered in different mists. Ducks huddled in three separate groups. At the north side of the pond, a kingfisher was diving along its sight line, then returning to its branch, sometimes with a fish—diving, returning, diving, returning.

But I noticed that the kingfisher on the western shore, whose perch was a craggy branch of an old lightning-struck maple, was not sitting upright like an exclamation point, which would be normal. Instead it wobbled, tucked itself between trunk and branch as if to gain balance, before tentatively venturing out along the length of the branch to resume its scrutiny of the pond. Something was a little off there. An hour later, when I mentioned this to the young woman working summer hours at the Maple Corner General Store, Octavia, who was majoring in biology at college, she said, "My uncle takes his lunch break by that part of the pond. Maybe he emptied his flask of whiskey into it." The local conservation officer, Dave, who had stopped in for a coffee, eavesdropped and took things literally. "Tell him to stop doing that," he said.

Experienced friends had warned against contracting the Benidini Brothers, but for two weeks after the kitchen faucet started to dribble silt, they were the only well-drilling concern to answer the telephone. I'd read in the *Times-Argus* that business for well drillers was booming. Our neighbor Scott had unloaded from his pickup three barrels of water for general use. We were taking baths and showers in a house in nearby Plainfield. On my way back from the millpond, I stopped at Legarre's Produce to purchase plums, melons, peaches, corn on the cob, bottled water, and strawberries. Driving up Peck Hill Road, I saw the top of the well-drilling rig. It towered the way you might see a giraffe's head and neck in the distance when you enter through the gates of a zoo.

Six men — including three well drillers — stood on the lawn. One was the road commissioner, Roy Bolz, who in height and weathered handsomeness had an uncanny resemblance to the writer Peter Matthiessen. Roy often won backhoe competitions at state fairs; he could set a peach down on a fence post with his backhoe. A videocassette recording of this feat was available for borrowing at the post office, which had an ad hoc lending library, too, mostly used paperbacks, including a couple of books I'd written. The town historian, Earlene Leonard, who kept track of such things, had said to me, "The movie of Roy gets signed out way more often than your books. Take my word for it."

I walked up to the giant Erector set that was pumping away, slamming into the earth with percussive thuds I'm sure could be heard half a mile away. "They're at two hundred eighty feet," Roy said. "My condolences." The Benidinis charged $2.50 a foot. Eventually, the well went down to 666 feet; to pay for it, I wrote six different articles, one for a magazine in Reykjavík, about having a well drilled.

Roy's word *condolences* seemed right; it did feel funereal on the lawn. Then everyone turned almost in unison to see my neighbor Maurice Persons, age sixty-six, who in younger days had worked in a granite quarry in Barre, walking slowly up the dirt road. Maurice had on the black greatcoat he'd worn in the quarry. In the heat-mirage distance, he appeared to have thickened into a bear, ambling in cartoonish ursine fashion as he approached. "He's got something under that coat," Roy observed, as if old Maurice were suddenly a menacing, nineteenth-century journeyman assassin for hire. "He's not that naturally wide."

When Maurice had gained my yard, he needed a breather. He looked over at the well-digging crew and said to me, "I've got a way to get these fellows off your property so we won't have to hold a wake for your bank account." At which point he opened his greatcoat like two vast wings, revealing a row of dynamite sticks in loop holders on either side of the lining. "You just toss a few of these into the old well casing, step back, and you have a new well," he said.

"I don't know, Maurice," I said. I had visions of my house collapsing into a sinkhole. "I just don't know."

123

"How old's that dynamite, anyway, Maurice?" Roy said.

"Good as new," Maurice said.

"I doubt it," Roy said.

One of the Benidinis, Jack, had dug a thin, shallow gulley through which sludge the thickness and color of cement runneled down the slope next to the house, and several tributaries had begun to flow toward the flower garden that I had to stop up with dirt. Jack checked the gauges on the rig; they relayed news from the underground. In an exhibit of annoying talent, Jack then ate an apple without using his hands. The apple turned in his mouth, and this made his brothers crack up with laughter.

Maurice walked back down the road, dynamite intact inside his greatcoat. "At one hundred fifty feet," Roy said, "they got some water, but it was surface water, it's called. It came out nice and clear, but it was soon gone. Even if a well's getting eighty gallons a minute, if the water's not clear, it's a bad well. They're into the kind of rock they like to see, though." Jack, who had been raking sludge, walked over and said, "The deepest we ever went was sixtwenty."

Olivia, who had been inside with Emma, appeared on the side porch and, making a gesture like she was holding a telephone to her ear, shouted, "It's for you."

I went in and picked up the phone and said, "Hello?"

"The Vermont-Canadian border is ninety miles," my brother said. "Lots of opportunity there."

I hung up.

This was the summer that our neighbors who didn't own a television set would walk up the road on some evenings to watch the Ken Burns documentary *The Civil War*. They would arrive with strawberries or rhubarb pie or sweet breads. We were all mesmerized by the episodes. They were titled "The Cause," "A Very Bloody Affair," "Forever Free," "Simply Murder," "The Universe of Battle," "Valley of the Shadow of Death," "Most Hallowed Ground," "War Is All Hell," and "The Better Angels of Our Nature." The heat was relentless, but we had fans set up to create a cross-breeze and made iced tea.

The documentary's soundtrack was all haunting fiddle and accordion music and ghostly voice-overs. Many letters from soldiers were read; the epistolary life during the Civil War, in sheer numbers of letters, endless ghastly anecdote, and tone of bewildered homesickness, was immeasurably heart-wrenching. Each line of printing or cursive shown in close-up on the screen, each of the hundreds of black-and-white photographs, contained history. Many of the photographs depicted battlefields, often with numerous bodies strewn in twisted, agonized configurations that made for a kind of hieroglyphics of corpses, a forensic alphabet, especially when photographed from a hill or rise. Some of the individual dead looked as though they were merely sleeping. The voice-overs, the actual words of the soldiers, both Union and Confederate, got to me as easily as the photographs. The voices: each episode felt like a séance organized and directed by Ken Burns, and during my hours of watching, a powerful melancholy presided. Those photographs, though. The photographs were saturated, of course, with the sadness of a war that divided and ultimately defined us as a nation, but within that context also intensified our understanding of the uncanny power of photographs to haunt us.

Then, after a couple of hours, in the somewhat cooling air, the neighbors would set out up the road for home, a quarter of a mile away. It was as if we had all entered the mid-nineteenth century, the only ambient light being the moon and stars and the oil lanterns they held to see by. One morning at the post office, my neighbor Mark said, "Things in my house are getting strange. Allison and I stare out at the back field and imagine a battle going on."

The well took three full days to complete, and was, up to that time, the third-deepest private well in the state. I was writing those articles about having a well dug as fast as I could. I'm smiling as I write this now, but talk about pouring salt on the wound: When the Benidinis got to 620 feet, at about four p.m. on the third afternoon, I was looking at them through the lace curtains of my living room. It was like having my view filtered through a past century, as the lace was antique. I watched the oldest Benidini brother, Toby, strip off his T-shirt, walk to the auxiliary tank of water (used to reduce friction), pick up a plastic container, fill it from the tank, and pour water from it over his head. He then took out a bottle of shampoo — the kind you get in hotel rooms — and proceeded to shampoo his hair, then rinse it with what water was left in the container. Taking a comb from his back pocket, he styled his hair into a duck's-ass. I must've been at wits' end, because his casual use of water set me off, to the point where I was going to comment on it through the window screen. I have no earthly notion what I would have said, but I never got around to it, because the telephone rang.

"I really need to get into Canada," my brother said. "I saw a suspicious car in the motel parking lot. A man got out and walked to a diner. I went over for a look at his car. There were binoculars on the front seat. Believe me, he didn't look like any bird watcher."

"You're having paranoid delusions."

"I understand you haven't heard from me for a couple of years, but you're hearing from me a lot already this summer. See? People can change."

"You're putting me in a very difficult position, here."

"The problem with you is, you can't grant your brother a simple favor. Know what I'm doing right now? I'm closing my eyes and seeing us crossing the Canadian border."

"You've got movies in your head."

"How about this for an idea? A picnic a hundred yards before Canada. Little Emma points and says, 'Dada, what's that?' And you say, 'Honey, that's the Canadian border. After our picnic is over, your uncle Mike is going to walk right across it. Won't that be fun to watch?' Let me add something to the bargain. I give you full permission—and I'd sign a piece of paper to this effect—*full permission* to use this incident in a novel."

"So you're providing me with ideas now."

"Somebody has to."

"I try to do that for myself."

"Good luck. I still hear those well diggers in the background. Which reminds me, know what's weird? Whenever I try talking sense to you, I get parched. This amazing thirst. When I hang up I'll probably drink ten glasses of water in a row. Have you thought about my offer?"

"Stop calling collect, okay?" I hung up.

Then the Benidini Brothers started to dismantle their giant Erector set. Just like that, it was over. I went out onto the side porch and said, "What's going on now?" Toby said, "We've stopped at five gallons per minute. But it'll improve as things open up even more where we've cracked rock deep down." It took the next two hours for them to dismantle the rig, load it on the flatbed. The last thing Toby said was, "We'll accept payment in three installments. You didn't ask for that arrangement, but this hole went very deep. You know, we'd rather have something in pocket right up front."

I wrote a check for the whole amount. The next morning I went into town to get new typewriter ribbons. Two of the articles on well drilling were due in ten days.

Conversation with my brother, June 27:

"It's four a.m.," I said.

"Oh, sorry. It's only two where I'm calling from."

"That narrows your location down to the western United States."

"You don't sleep much anyway," my brother said, "if memory serves."

"I take it—in the legal sense—someone is looking for you?"

"Nice to be wanted, isn't it?"

"That would make me laugh if it was funny."

"So here's my offer. I come and spend some quality time with my new niece, whom I haven't yet seen. Then one night you drive me up to Canada. I'll fall right out of my bind."

"Well, have you given any thought to the fact that I'd be aiding and abetting a criminal? You want my daughter to have a father in jail? That'll make me an absent father. I'm not in that family tradition. What is your legal *bind*, anyway?"

"The less you know the better. I'll pay for a full tank of gas, don't worry about that. How long do you need to consider my offer?"

"Ten years."

I hung up, or he did.

. . .

In the middle of July I went to an owl conference held in Wolcott, Vermont. Owl specialists from all over the world attended. In the evenings, and through the night and early-morning hours, some participants went out looking for owls in nearby Great Bear Swamp. All the heavy-duty flashlights had been bought up from local hardware stores. One ornithologist from Japan bought a miner's helmet, and its beam funneled yellow-white light up into the trees.

On the second afternoon of the conference, a Frenchwoman, Dr. Joubert, gave a lecture with a title she said had been inspired by François Villon, "In the Darkness Where the Dreaming Begins," in which she described what was for her the dreamlike quality of seeing owls on a moonlit night. Her paper also contained esoteric references, but it distinguished itself by its ethereal tone, especially since the majority of lectures were incredibly dull. Still, even in the paper titled "Parasites in the Great Horned Owl" there was something interesting to learn. Besides, it wasn't every day you got to be with people obsessed by owls.

After Dr. Joubert's lecture, a picnic dinner was served on the newly mowed common, big as a football field, at Craftsbury Common. It proved to be a beautiful evening and night, a vast array of stars with a gibbous moon presiding. After dinner, a dozen or so conferees, a veritable parliament of owl aficionados, slathered in mosquito and blackfly repellent, set out for Great Bear Swamp. I stopped at the library of the Center for Northern Studies to take my temperature. For some reason, it had spiked to 101.5. But the later and cooler it got, the more the night air would be a balm, and anyway, I was eager to see owls.

On another day, breakfast at the local diner. A meandering drive on back roads. Working on a new novel during hours that the

Marshfield Library is closed, with Emma napping in the portable car seat in the children's books section. Crows in the conifers across the street. The phone rings in the library's empty office. Many paragraphs typed on the Olivetti manual, a few kept. Everything I loved most happened most every day. With the exception that, when I got home, I found a note: *Your brother called. Wouldn't leave a return number. Will call later.*

At dusk, the barred owl flew out the door of our three-story barn, glided over the near field, then disappeared toward the lower field and woods. I don't know what was behind my impulse to name this owl, but I named her Gertrude. (In 2003, I named her successor in the barn Edna.) That evening, after watching the "Forever Free" episode of *The Civil War*, I could not sleep, so I went outside and walked to the two-lane, Route 14, where usually I'd go up the curving road in order to look back, my favorite view of the house. I stopped in front of Maurice and Kay Persons's red ramshackle house with its slumping porch. The lights were out. (Maurice once admonished me for leaving too many lights on in my house at night. "Electricity adds up," he said.)

The night was very still. I heard a loud rustling of some sort—raccoons, I thought, but then there was a rush of air, then nothing. I swept my flashlight beam across the open garage adjacent to the house. There was Gertrude, sitting on a wooden shelf above Maurice's black greatcoat on its nail; she had a vole dangling from her beak, a trickle of blood on its fur. I never realized before just how enormous a bird this was. I turned off the flashlight and immediately Gertrude whooshed past less than a foot from my head. It made me duck and throw my hands in front of my face. Off she went as if following the moon-illuminated dirt road up to our barn. I knew that this would never happen again. But part of what I loved most every day was thinking about this incident every time I walked or drove past Maurice's house. Yet another place along this dirt road had become a mnemonic.

The next morning, another neighbor, Allison, dropped by to say that their grey-and-white cat, Pemberton by name, had gone missing. "She's disappeared for days on end before," Allison said. "But we're asking people to keep a lookout. She's got a collar with a name tag and phone number and everything."

The Independence Day parade in Cabot. The Bread and Puppet troupe led things off, with its founder, Peter Schumann, dressed as Uncle Sam on stilts, and timeless antiwar slogans in ten-foot-wide sheets held between poles by giant, doughy-headed puppets. Ironically, next in line came a dozen World War Two veterans. The breast pockets of their ill-fitting uniforms draped with medals, these elderly men walked slowly and waved to the crowd on either side of the street.

I'm eating a cherry-cheese danish at Rainbow Sweets Café, talking about books and Russian classical music with the proprietor, William Tecosky. Gabrielle Deitzel up on a ladder at the back of the farmhouse, taking down last year's paper wasps' nests to use for an art project. Standing in the waist-deep water of the creek at the bottom of the dirt road, fingerling trout brushing past your knees. Kestrels, hawks, crows, sparrows, robins, towhees. At night, fireflies hover above the garden along the stone wall. I look out over the field and see thousands more. The eyes of deer rising and falling in the near dark. The radio tuned to the BBC at midnight, but of course there's the overseas time difference. Which means the European workday has already arrived at my house. Time travel by radio.

· · ·

I thought back to the last day of well drilling: the giant rig with its insatiable thirst in the drizzling rain. The well diggers, on lunch break, had gone to the diner in Hardwick, a depressed little town but with a lovely bookstore and a café. I put on my raincoat and went out and measured the old well by dropping a flat stone on the end of a thread, then measuring the thread. In about an hour the diggers returned and bivouacked under a tarpaulin. The noise of the equipment was muffled by the rain. Inside on the kitchen table, Jane had left a note: *Handel's "Water Music" on VPR tonight.* I could almost laugh. Rain on the roof in a soporific cadence. I wanted to take a yearlong nap.

The telephone rings.

"It's mail fraud and tax evasion."

"You've been busy."

"What they call white-collar crimes."

"Will it be Terre Haute prison again if—?"

"*If* what? If you don't take me into Canada *if.* That's the only *if* you should be thinking about."

"I have to say no. I'll drive you to a border crossing. It's on a back road. But I won't take you over. Anyone asks, I can say I didn't know you were, um, under legal duress."

"Since you were a kid, you thought if you used words cleverly, people would think you're clever."

"I don't think anything of the sort."

Then, out of nowhere, he said, "I read fifteen poems by Robert Frost last week. Doesn't sound like me, does it? *Fifteen.* And after fifteen of them, I thought, Robert Frost is loyal to things. He's loyal to the truth. And I further thought, If Robert Frost had a brother in need, he'd fix up a horse and sleigh and take that brother through hellfire and ice storms into Canada. He lived in Vermont some of the time, in case you didn't know."

"What would you do in Canada?"

"Not live in the U.S."

"Meaning they won't extradite you for the kind of thing you screwed up with."

"So my attorney tells me."

"You have an attorney?"

"I call him that. He studied law in Terre Haute, the prison library. He's more a legal adviser, I suppose. I advise him about certain things in return."

"I bet. Well, why not advise him to drive you into Canada?"

"What happened to us, anyway? We used to be so close when you were three and I was six, remember?"

Early on the evening of July 20, feeling somewhat better, I drove to Plainfield to have dinner alone at a café. I sat by a window and looked out at the Plainfield United Methodist Church across the street. Restaurants and cafés had come and gone in Plainfield, and this present one struck me as doomed, but the food was good. Olivia had come to the house to babysit while Jane worked on some writing for a couple of hours. The evening before, we'd watched the "Simply Murder" episode of *The Civil War*.

In the café I ordered cold cucumber soup and bread. There was only one other customer, a woman in the volunteer ambulance crew out of Marshfield. She was eating the cucumber soup with bread, too. We nodded hello and she went back to reading her magazine. My table was in the path of a floor fan, which helped, but I was definitely feverish again. After a few spoonfuls of soup, I picked an ice cube from my water glass and rubbed it on my forehead. This fever thing was getting scary. Casting over my unscientific inventory of worst-case scenarios, I decided I had tetanus, but couldn't remember whether I'd stepped on a nail earlier in the month out in the barn or just dreamed it. I wrote a few letters by hand. I jotted something in a notebook. Then I stared out the window for a while. The waitress had nodded off at a corner table; neither of her customers had any need to wake her. The radio was playing the soundtrack from *The Civil War*, which had become popular.

At dusk I watched as the AA meeting let out from the church basement. It was a Thursday; everyone knew that's when the AA meeting took place. Most of the AA people seemed reluctant to leave and stood around talking, lighting cigarettes in the courtyard inside the stone wall. It was at that moment I saw — or thought I saw — a Confederate soldier who was in the *Civil War* documentary. This couldn't be true, but I didn't immediately credit my fever with making it seem true. I was too lost in his face. And what was stranger yet was the fact that I knew the exact photograph he had appeared in, one taken by Alexander Gardner. In that photograph, a Rebel soldier — this same man — sat in haggard despondency near a stone wall as Union soldiers stood nearby in a tight circle smoking cigarettes, their bayoneted rifles propped against the wall not ten feet from their prisoner.

The man I "recognized" broke from the AA group and, with a slight limp (I thought, War wound), sauntered across the street and stood in front of the café window, where I got a closer look at him. He was probably in his late forties, with deep crow's-feet at each eye. He was tall, with a gaunt face, wispy beard, and unusually thick eyebrows. He stood there for about ten minutes. While the other dozen or so AA participants got into cars and drove off, this man walked from town up toward Maple Hill. As it happened, our waitress had woken up and come over to ask if I needed anything else. She had been born and raised in Plainfield. "Sandra," I said, "did you see that guy smoking a cigarette just now, right out front here?"

"Of course I did. He was right on the sidewalk. Sure, I saw him."

"Do you know his name?

"He's not from around here, at least not Plainfield. Did he come from the AA meeting?"

"Yes, he did. Definitely, he did."

She set down my check and went back to the kitchen.

I continued to frequent the millpond, sometimes three times a week, and had alerted people at the Nature Conservancy and other environmental organizations about the peculiar behavior of the kingfisher. I was certain it was in trouble. When I didn't get much response from those sources, I telephoned a friend who worked in the ornithological laboratory at Cornell University. She listened to my description of the kingfisher's behavior and said, "Well, it's still alive, which means it's catching fish. It's surviving so far. That's good. My guess is some sort of parasite." She called the Vermont Agency of Natural Resources, and two state biologists met me a couple of days later at the millpond. While waiting for them, I took my temperature—100—and stripped down and took a quick swim, then saw their truck coming up the road.

The two biologists, a man and a woman, introduced themselves. The woman climbed right up the lightning-struck maple and, using specially made padded tongs, clasped the weakened kingfisher and gently brought it to the ground. "Obviously, I couldn't have caught this bird if it was in tiptop shape," she said.

"We'll run some tests and get it back here as soon as possible. There's a hawk and a crow ahead of it in the lab, but it won't take but a day or two." Off they went in their truck.

I kept my sightings of the Confederate soldier to myself—after all, it was *my* dispute with reality—but I saw him on the following dates: July 23, walking past Country Books in Plainfield, near the Plainfield United Methodist Church; July 27, dressed in the same clothes he had on the evening of the AA meeting, and smoking a cigarette in front of the Plainfield fire station; and July 29, walking out empty-handed from the Plainfield post office. That same evening, I saw him walk by the front of the café in Plainfield and again head toward Maple Hill; this time he was wearing a Confederate soldier's cap. (I thought, Yeah, but so what? I've seen those for sale at the army-navy store on Route 2.) I'd noticed a Goddard College student sporting one just a few weeks earlier. Still, I made an appointment with a psychotherapist in Montpelier.

Lost Cat notices with a photograph of Pemberton were displayed on every general store, post office, and food co-op bulletin board in the area—cats can wander surprising distances. Rural Vermont cat stories could fill a thousand-page anthology. There was a story about a cat in Woodbury that had leaped into the back of a UPS truck only to be discovered when the driver was unloading boxes 150 miles away. Another story told of a cat in Danville that had somehow wedged itself into a cubbyhole in an enormous barn; its owners could hear it yowling, but because of the peculiar acoustics of the barn—this also occurred during days and nights of thunderstorms—could not find the cat itself. A full week passed, and the voice of the cat grew weaker. Early one morning, the family's fifteen-year-old daughter looked up and saw a cat's tail waving out from a hole. The cat had somehow positioned itself so as to flag its location.

Yet another cat story: A cat had wandered away from a campsite in Groton State Forest. Its owners, a young couple, saw it scamper up an oak tree, and they walked along below it, following the cat as it leaped from tree to tree at various elevations for a good long way. Then it disappeared in the treetops. The couple moved their campsite. For two days and nights they did not see the cat. After searching for another full day, they decided to go to the general store in Marshfield to get some food and bottled water. Not about to give up hope, they returned to their original campsite and set up their tent there. In the morning, the woman opened her eyes to find the cat sitting on her chest.

Then there was the Russian blue communally owned and cared for by the fire department of a small town in southern Vermont. The cat had curled itself up inside the folded American flag that was raised every morning on the pole in front the station. When a rookie fireman raised the flag, the cat, its claws clinging to the cloth, went up with it. The rookie figured that all he needed to do was lower the flag and the cat would be rescued. By now the entire fire crew was watching, along with various townsfolk. When the rookie began to lower the flag, the cat removed itself to the rounded top of the flagpole, precariously holding on for dear life. But the moment he saw the cat transfer itself to the pole, the fire chief ordered his crew to hold trampoline-like safety nets around the pole, and just in the nick of time, because the cat plummeted, landing uninjured on one of the nets, at which point it jumped from the net, walked into the fire station, and began to drink from its water bowl.

. . .

From my first appointment I decided that the therapist would not be much help. I doubted that I actually wanted to get to the heart of the mystery. Moreover, I think I wanted the Confederate soldier to be some sort of representation, or verification, of the astonishing sadness my neighbors, my family, and I felt while watching *The Civil War.*

"We see what we wish to see sometimes," Dr. ____, the therapist, said after I'd described my Confederate ghost to him.

"If that's the case, it's about time I had a wish come true," I said. I felt as if I were channeling my older brother's snide tone, his predisposition toward a lack of basic civility.

"Okay," he said, undaunted. "Here's an idea. Why not go looking for this man. This Confederate soldier. Set up a kind of surveillance, dedicate yourself to finding him like a detective might. Or hire a detective. I could give you some names. Track this man down, and if you find him — according to your many recent sightings he's in the Plainfield area. If you find him, just ask him his name. He might be offended, but he might be . . . civil."

I didn't laugh at the pun.

"Despite the two of us being total strangers," I said.

"Well, he has become quite *familiar,* though, hasn't he? Though it's one-sided."

"I could say, 'You are the spitting image of a Confederate soldier in the Ken Burns documentary about the Civil War.'"

"Yes, be direct. He might be interested. What's the worst that could happen?"

"Well, I imagine . . ."

"Let me put it differently. What would you like to happen?"

"I'd like him actually to be a Confederate soldier."

"All right. All right, well. Yes, that would explain why he's at an AA meeting. Post-traumatic stress disorder — from, say, Gettysburg. Didn't you say that in the photograph he was a prisoner of war?"

"Poor guy. First he had to travel north to Vermont, then he had to wait until Alcoholics Anonymous came along. I think you're humoring me."

"On the contrary. I'm trying to find a way to talk about this."

"Me too."

"Why else, do you imagine, would you want him to be the real thing? Maybe because—and I've been watching it, too—the documentary is all photographs and the disconnected voices of the narrators. Yet you saw an actual physically present person outside the café, correct?"

My time was up. With the little I had left over from paying the Benidini Brothers, I paid for this session—things are done informally in Vermont—with an envelope of cash. That seemed fine all around.

Late one very hot morning, I was driving, Emma in her car seat, to see if the kingfisher had been returned to the millpond when, up ahead on Pekin Brook Road, I saw a car pulled over to the side, near the creek. The trunk was open, the spare tire was on the ground, and the man, who turned out to be my new therapist, was studying a sheet of paper, presumably to learn how to work the jack and lug wrench.

I pulled up behind his car, turned off the ignition, got out—Emma had dozed off—and said, "Hello, Dr. _____."

"I've got a bad back," he said. "Ruptured a disk some months ago. Would you mind?"

"Not at all, not at all. Glad to help." I got the car jacked up, changed the tire, put the lug nuts on finger tight, lowered the car, fully tightened the nuts, and tossed the jack and the flat tire in the trunk. "That's that," I said. I didn't mention that I was the least mechanically adept person I knew. Still, I could change a tire.

"Thank you. You weren't by any chance heading over to Plainfield, were you? To look for your Confederate soldier?"

"Not today. But I think your idea is a good one. I'm going to follow up on it."

"Make another appointment if you're so inclined."

Next, I stopped to watch Viiu Niiler and Chet Cole blow glass, shaping it into vases, plates, and decorative sun catchers. I sat on the steps of their studio and we had a conversation while they worked. Then I stopped in at Country Books, where I discovered that a friend of mine had sold to the proprietor, Ben Koenig, a rare two-volume set of the paintings of Matisse, with commentary by the French poet Louis Aragon. I had loaned these books to the friend a month earlier, because she had wanted to study Matisse's paintings for inspiration for her pottery. I bought back the two volumes. A week or so later, Ben informed me that my friend had dropped by to "study" the Matisse volumes. "I trust you didn't tell her I bought them," I said. "She'd be embarrassed." Yet I could see from the look on his face that Ben *had* told her; etiquette is different for different people.

I next stopped at Cabot Greenhouse and purchased six Japanese crabapple trees. While running errands at two general stores, a gas station, a hardware store, and Legarre's Produce, I saw *Lost Cat* notices for Pemberton. I took my temperature about a dozen times during the day; it ran the gamut between 99 and 102. Now that I think about it, it must've looked odd to customers at Rainbow Sweets Café: here was a man with a piece of poppyseed cake and a cup of coffee on the table in front of him, reading a book of poems by W. S. Merwin with a thermometer in his mouth.

That evening, during dinner at Roy and Gabrielle's, Jane jokingly said, "We've been getting along really well with our fevers." Later, everyone watched the "War Is All Hell" episode.

"Hello."

Silence a moment. Then my brother said, "I don't hear the noise anymore. That well must've run you into the thousands. What's the worry, since your last book made millions."

"Sure, right, of course it did. A fledgling literary novel set in northern Manitoba. It was ten weeks on the northern Manitoba bestseller list."

"Per word, what do you make, approximately, per word?"

"It doesn't work that way."

"That's too bad. A dollar a word, say, would be pretty good. Though you'd have to learn to write long books, right?"

"Right."

"There's only an hour's time difference between us now."

"I take it you're in the Midwest."

"See, right there, what you just said. Very astute. You should write a detective novel. You'd probably make some real money. I've had certain experiences. I could be your ghostwriter, I think they call it."

"No, a ghostwriter is someone who actually writes the whole book but remains anonymous. They put somebody else's name on the cover."

"That wouldn't bother me."

"Which way wouldn't bother you—if you were the ghostwriter or you were the one taking credit?"

"Holy God in heaven, how does your wife put up with you more than an hour at a time? You have to dissect everything like it's a frog in high school biology class. What a dunce. If there was a stool in the corner of Vermont, you should go sit on it with your dunce cap on."

"It's five a.m. and you called collect."

I hung up and drove to the millpond.

On an evening in mid-August, the Confederate soldier and I were the only customers in the café in Plainfield. He was already sitting at a table when I arrived. He had his visored military cap on. It freaked me out, I have to admit, seeing him like that. I might have turned around and fled but for the fact that Sandra, the waitress, said, "Hey, I told this guy you're a local writer. He's a Civil War buff and I directed him over to Country Books." She turned to the Confederate soldier. "Right?"

"That's right," he said.

I sat down at my table.

"This cap must look kinda stupid," he said. "I'm trying to stay connected to my son."

"How's that?"

"Well, I've rented a place up Maple Hill here. My son is eighteen and his summer job is being a Civil War reenactor down in Virginia. He's learning a lot and we get to talk about that. He's dying once a day, twice on Saturdays and Sundays, for the tourists. But I think the job's getting to him. It's sinking in what actually went on during the Civil War. It's getting to him."

"I've been watching the Ken Burns documentary."

"Me too."

"I saw you earlier this summer, over in the church courtyard across the street."

"Oh yeah? I go to meetings there."

"I thought—this will sound crazy. I thought you were right out of the Ken Burns documentary. You bear a striking resemblance to a Confederate soldier in it."

"The mind plays tricks, huh?"

"You aren't kidding."

"And then you find out my kid's doing reenactments. Synchronicities or what?"

"Synchronicities. By the way, I'm Howard."

I walked over and we shook hands. "St. John Holman," he said.

I left the café without ordering a meal. Later, it was as if I knew the exact moment my fever broke. It was about one a.m. I was in the kitchen listening to the BBC. I took my temperature: normal. I took it again at two a.m. and right after waking at six-thirty a.m.: normal.

Earlier in the summer, back at the owl conference in Wolcott, at about three or four o'clock in the morning, the group scattered out in the swamp, quiet, listening for owls. I was standing with a Frenchwoman named Dr. Ponge when she brought her flash-light close to my face and said, in a thick accent, "Do you mind if I . . . ," and placed the palm of her hand on my forehead. "I think you have malaria," she said. Malaria was obviously a stand-in for a high fever; she didn't mean malaria literally. "I've been looking at you, and your eyes look . . . rheumy. I think you should go home and lie down. You live in Vermont—you can come to this place anytime, yes?"

I took out my small leather case that had the thermometers inside. Standing in the muck, surrounded on all sides by an international array of owl obsessives, I took my temperature. "Let me read it," Dr. Ponge said. She studied the thermometer. "Oh, okay—okay, not good. Not good."

I walked out of the swamp, got in my car, and drove to the main building of the Center for Northern Studies. I took two bottles of spring water from the small refrigerator and drank them both in short order. I lay down on the cot in the auxiliary room and fell right to sleep. When I woke and looked at the clock on a nearby worktable, it read 11:05 a.m.—I'd slept for approximately seven hours.

When I made my way to the conference room, I found Dr. Ponge and five or six other people looking at photographs of Asian fishing owls. "Oh, we had a doctor come out—do you remember?" Dr. Ponge said. I said I didn't remember that at all. "Yes, he examined you and took your temperature. It was down to almost normal. So he said to just let you sleep. And by the way, I spoke with a young woman who answered your telephone. Olivia. I told her you were sleeping and there were a lot of people here, and that there was nothing to worry about. Olivia said she'd give the message to your family, okay?"

"Well, thank you so much for looking after me. I didn't mean for that to happen."

"No problem," she said. Then everyone went back to the photographs.

"Did you see many owls last night?" I asked.

"Yes, quite a few," Dr. Ponge said. "It was very satisfying."

Late in the evening on the day the owl conference ended, I went into my barn after dinner and, on the hay-strewn floor of the upper level, beneath the rafter beam on which Gertrude could most often be observed, I discovered Pemberton's name tag.

This was really confusing. Looking up at the rafters, I imagined the bones of Pemberton, his skull perhaps, and tufts of fur; in the past I'd climbed up there and seen the skeletal remains of mice, wood rats, snakes, hares, fish, toads, and birds. Allison and Mark had two young sons; the family adored Pemberton. How could I tell them? *Should* I tell them? What was the right thing to do in these circumstances? Mark worked for the Nature Conservancy; that he surely knew all about predator-prey relationships was one thing, but that their beloved pet had been lifted into the air, carried aloft to the rafters of my barn, and eviscerated by a sharp beak and talons was quite another. I'd had the passing thought, too, that the boys, who each owned a .22-caliber rifle, might naturally seek revenge on Gertrude. In every important regard they were solid boys, but still, one could hardly blame them.

In the end I never uttered a word. In subsequent years my family lost several cats, who simply never came back from nighttime wanderings. After each disappearance, all of us were brokenhearted. I wondered if Gertrude had anything to do with those cats, but I stayed out of the barn for weeks, not wanting to know. And many times I'd see Gertrude flying from the paneless topmost window of the barn at dusk, and return at first light.

By the time I was exhausted from writing the next-to-last article on having a well drilled, I started the last one, for a magazine in California. I was allowed twenty pages. Reading that piece over now, I realize that to some extent it evokes a lot of the anxiety of that summer. The first sentence was, "We had set aside enough money to get through the summer but suddenly needed a new well dug, which meant we had not set aside enough." In the course of this article I shamelessly depicted the Benidini Brothers as deviously clever white trash, and suggested that people were at their "mercy" in every aspect of well drilling, from the location of the well itself to taking their word for "reading the water," as it was called, meaning its volume and clearness. Of course, all of that was simply my response to the nonscientific aspects of the profession of well digging. What is more, I inserted a dream about a neighbor's cat falling into a well. I also referred to another dream I'd had, of seeing Noah's Ark on the Winooski River, which ran through Montpelier. In the dream, Noah's wife was taking Noah's temperature with a modern thermometer. In rejecting the article, the editor of the magazine politely wrote, "These dreams are extraneous to the subject at hand."

Therapist: So, your fever broke right after finding out the Confederate soldier was not a Confederate soldier?
Me: Same night.
Therapist: No coincidence, then. There's much to talk about.

Everything I loved most happened most every day. While examining me again late in August, my physician said, "Just wanted to mention that I did some research into that mysterious fever you had. Not yours exactly, but mysterious fevers in general. I ran across one account of a man who had a temperature of a hundred and one for about twenty years, and one day it just dropped back down to normal. It was interesting reading. I have you to thank for that. Hope you're not disappointed, though, not getting into the *Guinness Book of World Records* or something. Okay, we're done here. You're good. Temperature's normal. Everything looks good."

I drove to Country Books. Ben Koenig's assistant said that St. John Holman had left town, but before he did, he purchased over five hundred dollars' worth of books about the Civil War, also a number of Civil War–era photographic postcards. "I helped carry it all to his truck," the assistant said. "Go back and look for yourself if you want. There's three completely empty shelves."

I went and looked. When I stepped up to the counter again, he said, "Know what else? I bought his hat from him for ten bucks. He got the good deal there." This assistant, who was about six feet tall, with a mountain-man black beard, who normally preferred to be inconspicuous, happy to labor away in silence back in the stacks, jauntily placed the Confederate soldier's cap on his head. It looked really stupid on him. "If you're looking for Ben, by the way, he's taking some time off. With that big sale, he might go to Paris."

On Vermont Public Radio, every forecast on the "Eye on the Sky" weather report dedicated itself to elaborate language, which some of my friends suggested was overkill. I didn't feel that way at all. I loved descriptions such as, "Southern portions of Quebec province sponsored last night's rain, and the same can be said about today's light showers throughout the broadcast area. Late-afternoon and early-evening waterspouts might hazard small craft on Lake Champlain. One farmer near Peacham reported geese had shown up in his barn. I suppose we shouldn't be surprised that even water fowl sometimes need to get out of the rain. Tomorrow, more rain. Temperatures will range between eighty and eighty-five in the lower elevations."

I stopped at Jules and Helen Rabin's house to pick up two loaves of bread they had made in their medieval stone beehive oven. On my way home I listened to Tom Slayton's excellent review of the latest collection of poems by Hayden Carruth and a retrospective of Carruth's writing life, and then switched off the car radio the moment I recognized the insufferable voice of Willem Lange, about to deliver a sanctimonious editorial. Then I noticed an enormous, prehistoric-looking snapping turtle crossing Route 14. I stopped the car, broke off a small branch from a fallen tree ten yards from the road, and approached the turtle, which spun to face me, hissing. The thing to do was get the turtle to lurch its accordion neck forward and bite the branch, then drag the whole contraption into the wet gulley alongside the road and run like hell. This worked out fairly quickly.

Late at night, I ate strawberries and cream, then watched the "Better Angels of Our Nature" episode. And I thought, This summer I've experienced my better and worse angels equally, and the summer isn't over yet.

By the end of August the kingfisher was back on its tree. I contacted the state biologist who had originally captured it. She said, "Yeah, just as I suspected, it was a parasite. It should be fine now, except sometimes just a short time away from home like that disorients a kingfisher. It might choose to change its tree. Which might not sound like much, but for a kingfisher it's major. Keep me posted. I'd be interested to know what's going on there."

Back at the millpond, I sat and watched both of the resident kingfishers. Splash to the west, then splash to the north, a kind of contrapuntal ornithology, and both birds were having much success. Then I saw that the kingfisher on the north side of the pond was in fact "teaching" a juvenile, perched on a nearby branch—I had read about but never observed this—to hunt. The way it works is that the parent bird will kill a small fish, then lay it on the surface of the pond. The offspring will then attack the fish, often missing it entirely, but occasionally spearing the fish successfully with its bill. This apprenticeship may go on for weeks and weeks. On this late-August day, the juvenile kingfisher was both picking up its mother's leavings and separately nabbing its own fish. I sat there for most of the afternoon. I wrote letters, read part of a friend's novel, took a nap, ate peaches. I hated to leave that beautiful place.

"I have only about three minutes," my brother said.

"Put in some more coins, then. Or—go ahead, call me collect. I don't care."

"No, I mean I'm *allowed* only three minutes. Get it?"

"Where are you?"

"Terre Haute, Indiana."

"I was wondering why I hadn't heard from you."

"There was a hearing. I didn't contest anything. They had me ass to ashes."

"I'll visit."

"It's for eighteen months. Definitely eighteen months."

"I'm sorry."

"I was wearing you down there, though, wasn't I? I could tell by your voice I was starting to work the magic. I mean, you'd agreed to take me to the border, if not across. Another week or two would've done it. I'm pretty sure."

"Maybe so."

"But be honest—you're kinda relieved it didn't come to that, right?"

"I don't know. What does it matter, anyway?"

"I haven't met your wife. I haven't met your daughter."

"When you get out, I'll come drive you to Vermont. You can visit us. I'll take you across all the state lines between Indiana and here. We can drive at night if it makes you more comfortable. That's about all I can offer, given the present situation."

"Time's almost up. I'm getting the look from the guard."

"Okay. Call collect next time if you want. Hope you'll be all right there."

"How *all right* can a person be in federal prison, ask yourself that. Though they do have—I mean, it's white-collar crime, minimum security. They do have therapists, priests, rabbis—they've got movies on one of those old-fashioned projectors. I'm thinking of doing some writing."

I had one last therapy session. "Do you want to continue to try and figure out the whole thing with the Confederate soldier?" Dr. _____ asked.

"I think I've been a little sick all summer. I was seeing things differently. I was feeling things differently."

"Did the confusion of it disturb you? It seemed to at times. The phone calls from your brother . . ."

"Not really. I didn't mind it. I got some work done. I got some bills paid. That well was goddamned expensive. I only fill up the bathtub halfway now, even though there's plenty of water. Saw a lot of friends. Saw five or six movies. I spent a lot of time with Emma."

"A normal summer with a few extra added attractions—is that how you prefer to see it?"

"I wouldn't put it that way."

"How would you put it?"

"The guy with the Confederate soldier's hat was . . . disappointing."

"You mean you wanted a ghost. You mean you wanted your fever to have put you in touch with a reality nobody else was in touch with. You wanted a summer of illness to have earned its keep somehow. To have provided you with a once-in-a-lifetime experience. But you are always saying how just everyday things here in Vermont sustain you so much. Actually, you know what? I don't see any real contradictions there. Not really. Howard, life contains disappointments."

"I know you didn't mean that to be as patronizing as it sounded. But the way you said it was kind of a dull platitude."

"Still, I meant it. Disappointment is a subject to discuss."

"I've always thought disappointment was in direct relation to expectations."

"So if you lower your expectations, disappointments arrive less often, or something like that. That's got some humor to it."

"I'm just saying I expected—fever or not—too much from the guy. It was enough that he looked very good in that hat."

"I can see you prefer to end on a light note. How unusual. Anyway, our time's up."

The night before I had to, and hated to, leave Vermont, because I had taken a teaching position in Maryland, I had a dream so vivid it made waking life seem a dream. Or something like that. I dreamed of all my friends asleep in their beds. Perhaps the influence was the fact that, before I'd fallen asleep myself, I'd read a poem by Mark Strand that contained the line "my friends asleep in their beds." It was a poem narrated by an insomniac, the image informed by vicariousness and desire. The poem began with a nighttime tour of bedrooms and sleeping porches of the poet's friends on a hot summer night.

Michael and Jackie asleep in their bed. Rick and Rhea asleep in their bed. Roy and Gabrielle asleep in their bed. Denise and François asleep in their bed in Paris. Chet and Viiu asleep in their bed. Alexandra asleep in her bed. David asleep in his bed in Venice. Gary and Vickie asleep in their bed. Kazumi Tanaka asleep in her bed. Richard and Jane asleep in their bed. Susanna and Larry asleep in their bed. David and Rebecca asleep in their bed. Ed and Curtis asleep in their bed. Julie asleep in her bed. Jerry and Diane asleep in their bed. Tom and Melanie asleep in their bed. Rick and Andrea asleep in their bed. David and Ann asleep in their bed. Bill and Trish asleep in their bed. William and Paula asleep in their bed. Elizabeth asleep in her bed.

I woke up, put on the BBC, and stepped out onto the dirt road at five a.m. Crows calling and the scuffle of deer in the direction of the trout pond, hummingbirds at the fuchsia. Gertrude was just returning to the barn. Can you imagine what comprises an owl's night? Already, the things I loved most every day had happened.

THE HEALING POWERS OF THE
WESTERN OYSTERCATCHER

~~

BOB EDWARDS
Morning Edition, NPR
12-16-2003

Bob Edwards, host: Imagine leaving home for the summer and while you're away, a terrible event occurs in the place you've left behind. That was the experience of some Washington neighbors of NPR special correspondent Susan Stamberg. Her Tuesday series, "No Place Like Home," continues.

Susan Stamberg: Novelist Howard Norman, his wife, poet Jane Shore, and their teenage daughter spend their summers in Vermont. This year they loaned their D.C. home to an acquaintance and her two-year-old son. This past July, in the dining room of that house, the woman committed suicide and took her little boy with her.

Jane Shore: At first, I was thinking, and we were all thinking, if we could actually go back home, and if we could actually live in the house, because it had been violated.

Susan Stamberg: So how was it? How did you then, Howard Norman, arrive at the idea that you, in fact, would go back to the house?

Howard Norman: I think that happened fairly quickly, actually. We agreed relatively quickly that this was visited upon us. It wasn't something whose source was our life, and that you don't let someone else's demon, if you will, chase you out. I came down a couple of days early, and I will say that it was a powerful feeling, to step into the house. The sense of relief at seeing the familiar life was quite astonishing, really, because one doesn't always like where one's imagination goes and the projection of it.

Susan Stamberg: And so it was so much more terrifying to think about it while you were out of town than to go back to what still was very much your house.

Truth be told, I scarcely knew Reetika Vazirani, and scarcely knew her son, Jehan, either. So if the word *healing* is applicable to working through the consequences of an act of unspeakable brutality, it wouldn't be associated with grieving. Grief is reserved for loved ones. In this situation, healing was about other imperatives, such as reclaiming the violated interior spaces of heart and home, and gaining some perspective, in order to temper, if not erase, the harrowing images of what a person, Reetika Vazirani, suffering the consuming rages and ravages of depression, was capable of doing to her child and to herself, and of visiting upon my house.

Years earlier, and just days after we'd begun living in that house, I was attaching a mezuzah to the frame of the front door when Monsignor Duffy, of the Church of the Blessed Sacrament, whose rectory was next door—the church itself was across the street—dropped by to ask if I'd give a lecture before his Catholic

Book Club on the subject of "both real and delusional guilt in the novels of Graham Greene. I'd like a Jewish writer's perspective on a Catholic writer's philosophy, played out in the actions and thoughts of his characters." I told him that my lack of comprehension of this subject could only fail his book club. He let it go at that.

The bells of the church rang every fifteen minutes, seven a.m. to seven p.m., and of course more frequently on Sunday mornings, Christmas, Easter, and around weddings and funerals. I soon developed an antagonistic relationship with those bells. A friend described me as being like Quasimodo in *The Hunchback of Notre Dame,* up in the bell tower clamping his hands over his ears. The thing was, I was trying to get some writing done, needing several uninterrupted hours each morning, but the bells constructed never-changing allotments of time, often imposing a sense of anxiety on potentially meditative intervals. Jehan liked the bells, but they didn't always let him settle into a good nap, wrote Reetika Vazirani in a journal. Anyway, just now I'm thinking of something my therapist said: "Filicide strikes the deepest chords."

I wish I didn't have this subject to write about; every word will come out awkwardly and not suffice. But the fact is, the medical examiner determined that on July 16, 2003, Reetika Vazirani, a poet and forty years old, stabbed her son in the neck, chest, and forearm, damaging his blood vessels, lungs, and heart. Therefore, this was not, as the Indian poet Kabir wrote, "a gentle transport into the next world." And at that moment, too, a father, Yusef, lost his son — you wake up, as the Urdu poet Ghalib wrote, to find a demon standing on your heart. Next, Reetika Vazirani, by any definition, more gently transported herself.

How to talk about such a thing? Here I take as much inspiration as I possibly can from what Yasunari Kawabata wrote: "When speaking of those who take their own lives, it is always most dignified to use silence or at least restrained language, for the ones left most vulnerable and most deeply hurt by such an occurrence can feel oppressed by the louder assertions of understanding, wisdom and depth of remorse foisted upon them by others. One must ask: Who is best served by speculation? Who is really able to comprehend? Perhaps we must, as human beings, continue to try and comprehend, but we will fall short. And the falling short will deepen our sense of emptiness."

And yet sometimes I could not use restrained language.

"Reserving judgments is a matter of infinite hope," F. Scott Fitzgerald wrote. Still, I had to subscribe to some initial ways of looking at what had happened. To that purpose, the most incisively spiritual thing I read was a response by the poet Rita Dove to a journalist asking about Reetika Vazirani: "She couldn't find her way back to herself." And the most ethically useful thing was offered by David Mamet, who had driven over to our farmhouse in Vermont: "If you are walking down the road and you look up ahead and see a house on fire, if you are a good person you don't wish for it to be someone else's house." The essence of altruism in this felt meaningful, but I said to David that given the waking nightmare of a child murder, and the bewildered sobbing in my farmhouse, it was very difficult to feel much like a good person. He stayed for dinner to talk about it.

The summer had just been going along. Then on July 16, my family and a friend, Alexandra, had been to Montpelier, a twenty-minute drive from the farmhouse, for dinner at a restaurant. It was a balmy evening, and I remember pulling the car up to the house in dusky light and seeing a kestrel heliotroping over the slope of a dandelion-filled field, halfway between the garden along the stone wall and my writing cabin. Once inside the house, I lingered in the kitchen while Jane and Emma went upstairs to watch a movie. I'd intended to carry coffee and chocolate mints upstairs.

That's when I noticed the message light blinking on the telephone on the wall next to the pantry. It was one of those machines capable of archiving far more messages than one would normally receive during a few hours' absence from home. I pressed the button, put the receiver to my ear, and heard, "You have fifty-three messages." I got a bad feeling. I immediately poured a shot of Scotch; this could not be good news. Then, after hearing five police messages and one from friends, I went upstairs. Telling Jane, and aware that in the telling I would cause sadness, was like gasping for air. We waited until the next day to sit down with Emma and tell her what had happened.

Our dear friend Stanley drove up for a visit. Emma's pal Caitlin flew up and stayed for a week. Many wonderful people called from all over. It was a shocking irony to find out that in Washington, D.C., hearing the early reports of the incident in the distracted way we all take in local television news, a few people thought it was us who'd been murdered. In the face of this, my desperate, stupid joke was, well, if that had been the case, would I have answered the phone? I supposed I wanted to hear the relief in their laughter. But of course we were confused, discombobulated, our lives thrown radically off-kilter, and for weeks and weeks we had terrible, insomniac nights.

In the days that followed, the quotidian also served as blessed distraction: errands, house projects, Emma's Shakespeare rehearsals, city friends up for a visit, walks on the dirt road, swimming in ponds, attempting to write, the ten thousand things of daily life. But on some very basic level, an air of eerie if abstract preoccupation pervaded, and much of the emotional dimensions of familiar life had become unfamiliar. We were self-consciously aware of our need day by day to calibrate, adjust, and maintain our equilibrium. We carefully set about doing this. There were friends and laughter on those days and evenings. But at the same time, we held an ongoing vigil against despair, and as resourceful as we were, we knew we were amateurs up against a monstrosity. Falling apart, gathering life together, falling apart, gathering.

This odd thing happened with television in Vermont. I can far better understand it now, but at the time it was working on an altogether perplexing level. Jane started to watch reruns of *Law and Order* — mornings, afternoons, nights. These dramatic procedurals provided background visuals and voices (which sometimes felt like voice-overs of our own life, because to hear what the characters were saying, our silence was required) on the second floor of the farmhouse. I'd come and go, taking in snippets of dialogue and becoming generally apprised of plots and able to recognize the principal actors so splendid at portraying sanctimonious and brilliantly analytical detectives and scolds. Years later, when discussing this, Jane said that she was working on hope, and her thinking was that if she relentlessly exposed herself to the sheer plentitude and commonality of murder, it might somehow serve to anesthetize the pain of an individual homicide and "make things a little better." In episode after episode of *Law and Order,* the unifying reason for suspension of disbelief was that, with few exceptions, the murder was solved and the perpetrator brought to justice. Yet in messier real life outside of television, there had been the perverse miscarriage of justice in Reetika Vazirani's taking the life of her son, so as to "save him from a terrible world," a verbatim quote of the helter-skelter logic she advocated to herself more than once in her notebooks. Jane watched episodes of *Law and Order* for some time, until she realized that she'd begun to "retraumatize" herself, and so for the most part stopped.

But Jane wasn't alone in trying to find some way to invest in the possibility of allegory helping out a little. Over the next six months, I watched at least thirty times the classic cinematic treatise on child murder, *M,* directed by Fritz Lang and starring Peter Lorre. (I had not thought much about this movie since I was twenty, living in Halifax, when Isador Sarovnik regaled me with stories of his friendship with Laszlo Lowenstein.) But my successive viewings of this German expressionist film only served to transfer the real-death images — for example, those in the police photographs taken in our dining room — to the cinematic depiction of child murder. Not much help there at all, really.

Emma had turned fifteen in April 2003. A wonderful pleasure to be with. She was a regular teenager, though I also knew her to have a big appetite for life and to be remarkably poised. Naturally, when the murder-suicide took place in July, that poise was shattered, but she got right to dealing with it. The morning after we received the news, she asked to go rowing on East Long Pond; I'd rented a cottage there for the summer. And that's what we did. She took up the oars and rowed herself and me the mile or so circumference of the pond. And whether consciously or not, she rowed with fierce concentration and at a fast pace, her face flushed with exertion, her arm and leg muscles straining, and I mean without cease, until we returned to the dock. Once we had overturned the rowboat on land and begun to walk up the wooden steps of the cottage, I looked at her and thought, My daughter's going to be okay.

I felt right then, and feel the same way now, that this seemed entirely consistent with Emma's dignified comportment, and that it showed a lot of self-knowledge, too. I'd observed Emma at work in various darkrooms and could see that she loved knowing her way around them, and that she had already given herself over to a kind of parallel life in photography—that is, apart from school and the vexations and challenges of being a teenager. I can't really say that it was at that age she'd started thinking of herself as a photographer, but I knew that for her photography was definitely a passion. And while she could never have foreseen that the photographs she took of Jehan would all of a sudden become memorial portraiture—it was a fifteen-year-old's way of trying to entertain a two-year-old; they'd spent very little time together on the day he and his mother came to discuss staying in our house—she comported herself with thoughtful dignity: Emma developed the negatives but in the end decided against making prints.

It is important to say again that I scarcely knew her. I didn't at the time and don't now care to be informed about her biographical details. I've had quite enough of her life, which so violently intersected with my family's. We were friendly, but not friends. I admired some of her writing and even published three of her poems in an issue of the literary journal *Conjunctions* that I edited.

For a month or so before she took up residence in our house

in Washington, Jane had spoken with her on the telephone. My understanding is that Reetika Vazirani had called to ask about teaching jobs, but also indicated that most aspects of her life remained unresolved, including where she might live during the summer. Jane and I had been used to letting writers stay in the house. So it was characteristic of her empathy that Jane suggested Reetika Vazirani and her son Jehan might consider doing just that. No big deal, really. We were going to Vermont anyway, and it would be good to have someone look after things. For us it would be a *mitzvah*—the right thing to do. Personally, I had spoken with Reetika Vazirani only once before, at the Bread Loaf Writers' Conference in Vermont, and the topic of discussion on that occasion had been restaurants in Middlebury. The second time we spoke was when she stopped by in Washington to discuss housesitting.

On that visit, I had no sense of her taking any measure of the house at all: we sat in the living room drinking tea while Jehan watched a children's video upstairs in Emma's room. After exchanging pleasantries, she said, "A lot of writers said you were away in the summer, and we met once, remember?" Perhaps skeptical, certainly a touch edgy, I said, "Oh, a lot of writers. *Who?*" She reeled off a dozen or so names, and I thought: I don't know any of them. The initial discomfort on my part may have been caused by the fact that she was so deftly able to suggest the sponsorship of a very loose-knit literary community. But the thing was, when she started in on her domestic travails, I didn't grant much leeway. I felt that asking for a roof over her head was difficult enough without her having to test out various reasons. Besides, the most important reason was upstairs watching a video in my daughter's room.

How could I know? How could I know that the simplicity of our verbal contract—while living in our house you take care of it—might obfuscate future malevolence? Hindsight, of course, is powerfully suggestive and self-indicting, but cannot change what happened. Yet it has often occurred to me that had I let this weary-looking, jittery, and singularly accomplished woman with the lovely smile, whose intelligence I was, on the surface, beginning to enjoy, indulge in an hour or so of what I later understood to be a fugue state of exhaustion, fuming anger, self-pity, emotional claustrophobia, and God knows what else, I most likely would not have, at least in so perfunctory a manner, muted my protective instincts. I would have heard something alarming. In one breath I say, *How could I know?* and in the next breath say, *I should have known.*

Anyway, when she and I were done talking, I served more tea and brought out some carrot cake. We laughed over the photographs in a biography of Groucho Marx I'd been reading. Emma walked in the door, home from school, and immediately went upstairs to hang out with Jehan; she showed him her collection of key chains and took those photographs of him. I remember that, even without noticeably registering incipient concern, I felt some relief when mother and child left. I watched through the front window as they walked over to look at the Church of the Blessed Sacrament like tourists. Then I went upstairs to take a nap, or talk with Emma, or start dinner, I cannot recall. At the time, I was quite pleased, I believe especially on Jehan's behalf, but for both of them, that for a few months they'd have a cozy house where life could be lived, a playground nearby, a thousand books, a writing desk, light-filled rooms, classical music CDs in stacks, a rectory of Irish and South Asian priests next door.

From my mouth to God's ear, I wish I had said, "No, terribly sorry, but this housesitting situation isn't possible."

Reetika Vazirani had left a telephone message for Jane's best friend, Jody, to the effect that she was "in trouble" and to come to the house as soon as possible. Jody had barely known Reetika Vazirani either, but Jody had a key to the house. Given the amount of time between when the message was left and the murder-suicide took place, apparently Jody's assignment was to discover the bodies — can you imagine? — which Jody eventually did, and quickly alerted neighbors. The police and paramedics soon arrived. In a matter of hours yellow crime-scene tape covered both back and front porches like a garish Halloween prank. And as the investigation got under way, the news spread, and demons began to stand on a lot of hearts.

At the end of August, I flew down to Washington from Vermont and stepped into the house at about five-thirty in the evening. I had asked friends in advance to take down the three early-twentieth-century Dutch portraits hanging in the living room. The grim expressions on the Dutch faces had always struck me as judgmental almost to the point of satire, and I was convinced that these anonymous personages were witnesses and we shouldn't have to run the risk of seeing horror reflected in their eyes.

On the other hand, many gifts had arrived to redeem the walls. Antonin Kratochvil had sent one of his photographs. Jake Berthot had sent one of his exquisite drawings of trees. Kazumi Tanaka had sent her woodcut of Japanese cranes lifting from a pond. My friend Elizabeth had sent a photograph of the wild coast of British Columbia she had taken.

I opened a lot of windows, put an LP of Chopin's nocturnes on the old-school record player, and stood for a moment at the entrance to the dining room, looking at the new shellacked floorboards we'd ordered to replace the bloodstained boards. I looked at the houseplants that university colleagues had delivered. I set my Olivetti down on the dining room table. Facing the corner of the dining room where the bodies had been found, I began typing letters. I wrote to William in Hawaii; Stuart and Caren in Michigan; Rick and Rhea in Vermont; Bill and Trish in Vermont; Alexandra in Vermont; David in California; Mr. and Mrs. Malraux in Paris; Peter on Long Island; Jerry and Diane in California; my old ornithology professor Dr. Cleveland in Vancouver; Melissa Church in Seattle; Michael in Toronto; Deborah in Woodstock, New York; Michael, a portraitist of birds, in St. John's, Newfoundland; my college friend Richard in Florida; Mona in Paris; my mother, Estella, in Michigan.

I do not fully understand why I went on such an epistolary binge—all told, perhaps thirty letters, the briefest five single-spaced pages and some as long as twenty. Naturally, besides the fact that letter writing had always helped organize my emotions, I trusted that my friends would tolerate moodiness, outright despair, exhausted humor, philosophical nonsense, and everything else. I was drinking espresso after espresso; letters were stacking up next to the typewriter; I switched from Chopin to Bach's compositions for cello and works by Kodály, all performed by János Starker—with these selections I obviously was not seeking ebullience but rather an accompaniment to melancholy. Sleep was out of the question. Letter after letter after letter.

At around three a.m., with cicadas whining in the enormous tulip poplar tree in the front yard, which especially during high winds I had always felt was too close to the house, I was suddenly famished and—quite surprised to have an appetite at all—decided to make spaghetti, which in any season I considered comfort food. With the heat and humidity still coming in through the nighttime screens, I started to boil water in a big pot and took some spicy meatballs out of the freezer. I opened a bottle of red wine. The recipe would be makeshift. I emptied a can of tomatoes into a saucepan and added tomato paste and spices.

All of this had great possibilities, I felt, and then, as the saying goes, *right out of nowhere*—this is impossible to capture—I "felt" something was terribly wrong in the house. Not that something terribly wrong *had* occurred; needless to say, I already understood that. No, the definite sensation, but with an indeterminate source, was of something occurring. In progress. What is more, I had suddenly contracted a blistering headache. What else could I do but question my own exhaustion. Was I thinking clearly? What trick was my mind playing? No matter, no matter. I stopped cooking and—again, I cannot pinpoint the reason—was drawn upstairs to my third-floor attic study.

I switched on the desk lamp and immediately noticed a novel on the floor. I cannot recall the title, but the author was Penelope Fitzgerald. How odd, I thought, because whenever I left for the summer, I would without fail clear my desk, file away papers, put pens and pencils in a jar, everything neat and clean and in its own place. Yet here was a novel on the floor.

I picked it up and absent-mindedly flipped through the pages. I stopped at an arrow pointing from a passage Reetika Vazirani had underlined to her comment in the margin: *How could she write sentences like this? She should be pilloried on the TV news. It can't be forgiven.* I thought that this might have been laughable, evidence of a critical mind in high dudgeon or an exasperated bitchiness, yet given the circumstances, I had to sit down.

Turning the swivel chair to face the desk, I went through the novel page by page, discovering numerous underlined sentences and seemingly endless comments, some tactful and erudite, most expressing over-the-top outrage and dismissal of all worth. The inventory of suggested punishments for "poor sentences" was truly mind-boggling.

Sitting there, I happened to glance at the bookended line of upright black notebooks I had filled. Tucked in among them was a much smaller, squarish notebook. As I eventually discovered, this was one of thirty-three three-by-five-inch black notebooks that Reetika Vazirani had hidden throughout the house. Ultimately they required a macabre sort of treasure hunt whose negative reward was a gut-wrenching and permanently regretful reading experience. In that one notebook alone, amid drawings of Medusa heads, gargoyles, and clearly identifiable Hindu gods—some devouring children—were succinct rehearsals of the murder of her son, mentioning him by name. This writing was so penetratingly grotesque that all I could manage was to stumble down to the second-floor bathroom and vomit for a good half hour.

Given all this, it may sound unlikely to suggest that anything I found in one of her notebooks could offer the least solace. But as I knelt on the cold tiles (themselves soothing to the touch) I noticed, atop some magazines and books on a small shelf, a much larger blue notebook, a journal, and I opened it at random and read:

You have given me the greatest gift, to be led into a house full of light & comfort, paintings, photographs, cd's, tea, books books books I am at peace now.

This has been the greatest gift of all—to make a home like this

Perfectly suited for Jehan and me Two rooms to grow into
(top floor)
   5:30 up
   6:30 Yoga
   8:00 breakfast
   read & write
   1:00 lunch
   laundry
   4:00 Jehan napped till 7:00
   squandered most of the time piddling
   (a good day)

Which at first glance seemed addressed to my family, though it may have been a generalized, prayerful inventory. I just cannot know.

In that blue notebook—whose paper-clipped note cynically read *Save for Howard*—were theological and fantasy-erotic musings, literary quotations, accounts of dreams, arguments with a certain "Gremlin" (both sides of their dialogue recorded), professional to-do lists, domestic to-do lists. A lot of obsessive consideration was given to her "roller-coaster" experience of the humiliating vicissitudes and elusive rewards of a writing life: "My ambitions are poison." To her quoting of Borges's "Life is truthful appearances," she had added, "I prefer untruthful appearances."

After I had recovered a little—I was less dizzy and had gotten to my feet—my clearest reasoning was, if there are two such notebooks, there might be others, and if there are others, I had better try to find them. I started out frantically and without design, moving through familiar rooms but motivated by something both unprecedented and completely alien to my sensibility, and felt within minutes that I was more or less ransacking my own house. I sat on Emma's bed (where Jehan had slept), taking deep breaths and understanding the need to ratchet things down to a slower, more methodical pace — and then got down on my hands and knees and found a second three-by-five notebook under the mattress. The specific hostility implied in that placement sickened me all over again. I went down to the kitchen to drink a glass of ice water. When I opened the freezer compartment to get some ice, there was a notebook; I hadn't noticed it earlier, there amid the cartons of sorbet, sticks of butter, containers of pasta, and bottles of vodka.

I extended my search to the living room, where I found a notebook between two big books about Matisse I'd bought in Vermont. And inside the piano bench were three notebooks held together by a rubber band. Later, upstairs in the guest room, I found a notebook under a New Testament Bible she had borrowed from a neighbor. In the utility closet a notebook waited on top of the vacuum cleaner.

I cannot bear to complete this search in writing here, except to say that I saw and read enough in the first six or seven notebooks to be more than convinced that I did not want to know what was in the rest. In time — and I will get to this later — I realized that certain passages in these notebooks forced themselves into my memory. It was as if they had immediately graffitied themselves on a blank wall in my brain. These obscene, insistent mnemonics were in the form of sentence fragments and every sort of bizarre non sequitur, each with its resident aspect of malignant aphorism and disconnect:

I have a devotional nature but my eye pencil draws tarantulas; I'm a chameleon selling my face; God is at the height of pretentiousness

and balloon-faces shouldn't suffer that; take Pratma's Himalayan val-
ium in order to talk in rectangles; flee from the post-traumatic muse-
snatcher; Yoga didn't dispel biting trees; Lord I'm an unlucky detective;
sleep in the kitchen but running low of jars to fill with unhappy days;
nobody but me realized Buddha came back as a drawer; all gratitudes
are now Gremlins buying organic for the church. And: *inevitably I*
will derange my sanctuary.

At the end of that long day, did I suspect I would find more notebooks? There is no rhyme or reason to the fact that I didn't. I could have been quite wrong and my family may have suffered for it. I put the notebooks on the living room couch. It was still light outside. Through the window I noticed a few neighbors walking past, on their way to the bus or the Metro, or to the local Starbucks for a coffee, or breakfast at the diner.

I gathered the notebooks into five separate groups and wrapped each in sheets of newspaper sealed with Scotch tape. I hated these notebooks; I'd never hated anything so much in my life; I was deeply embittered by them; I was shaking. I took them outside and burned them to ash in the garbage can in the alley that ran between the rectory and my house. Peering through a window in the rectory, an Indian priest (in whom Reetika Vazirani had confided her mental precariousness; oh, had he only anointed Jehan with an intervention) watched the proceedings. A gaggle of kids on their way to Lafayette Elementary walked over to the garbage can. One boy said, "That's a pretty cool idea," as if I'd started a bonfire on a lark, and his buddy said, "Yeah, maybe I should toss in my stupid take-home quiz!" They went off down the block laughing and talking.

Unnerved but also definitely relieved, I went to the porch and sat for a while and listened to the staccato cooing of the pair of mourning doves that often perched next to each other on the telephone wire. When I went back inside the house, it felt as if I had reclaimed the very air — the light was lovely against the pastel floral patterns of the living room's overstuffed chairs and sofa. After half an hour of dreamless sleep, I awoke to a hopeful sense of lessened sorrow.

Before Jane and Emma returned to Washington, I sent a message to an ornithologist friend traveling in Arctic Canada around Hudson Bay to tell her what had happened. She responded right away to inform me that a Quagmiriut Inuit shaman named Petrus Nuqac, whom I had known decades earlier, was "still very much at work." To my astonished gratitude, two days later Petrus Nuqac flew by mail plane and jetliner from Churchill, Manitoba, to Winnipeg, to Toronto, and then to Washington, D.C. This was an arduous journey, especially considering that Petrus had never before boarded an airplane of any sort, let alone left the Arctic. Having traveled and sat in airports for much of a day and a night, he arrived by taxi at the house at about eleven a.m. Roughly seventy years of age, he was wearing blue jeans, a white shirt, shoes and socks, and a light brown sports jacket — "like a European," as he put it. His red-brown face was deeply furrowed. He had some English and I had some Inuit and we could communicate nicely.

After I served him scrambled eggs with lox, potatoes, and black coffee, we went out on the front lawn. On their lunch break, five or six girls from the parochial school, each wearing a uniform of plaid skirt, black shoes, and white blouse, stood on the sidewalk out front, curious as all get-out, as Petrus ceremoniously dug a hole and buried a caribou shoulder bone (how had he managed to get such a thing through customs?), traditionally used to fend off malevolent spirits, and offered a high-pitched, full-throated chant. Then Petrus and I sat on the front porch for a couple of hours.

A young parochial school boy, probably detouring from some assigned errand, stood on the bottom step leading up to the porch and said, "I heard you're an Eskimo." Petrus walked over to him and shook his hand and said, "It took me three airplanes to get here from Canada." I then called a taxi. And Petrus, carrying no luggage except a change of clothes in a plastic bag, left for National Airport.

Later in the autumn, Rabbi Gerry Serota and a few other close friends gathered in the dining room, and while there were no forms of exorcism in the Jewish religion appropriate to the occasion, Gerry had chosen compelling and beautiful Talmudic and Old Testament passages to read, and firmly instructed us to "not let someone else's sickness drive you from your own home." That is just how he put it, and I was grateful for his candor. It went pretty well, given the stressfulness and tears and not a little resurrection of unease, and it was nice to then have some food and drink in the living room and laugh it up a bit. What Petrus and Gerry had offered was poignant and necessary; we'd take every form of blessing we could get. That night I went back to typing letters at the dining room table.

There's a strong superstition in parts of Nova Scotia that if you want to keep unwanted ghosts out, and wanted ghosts in, you should place a pair of scissors crosswise so that it keeps an attic window shut. Seven or eight hours after the rabbi's houseblessing, I went up to my third-floor study and fixed a scissors crosswise in the small window, it being the topmost window of the house.

. . .

Some strange things happened in the aftermath. For a month or so after moving back to Washington, each time I arrived home from my university teaching after dark, as I walked up the steps I would experience a formal hallucination. Through the dining room window I would see a shadow-woman and shadow-boy in the midst of what resembled a Balinese puppet play, at once beautiful and tremendously disturbing. What is more, I would always arrive at the very moment when the woman raised her closed fist high above her head and in slow motion arced it down upon the boy as he reached out for her. Then the boy would fall from view. To my great surprise, after seeing this a few times I more or less got used to it. And then in March or April of 2004, roughly eight months after the murder-suicide, these shadow figures disappeared, permanently as it turned out, from behind the window, as if the house itself had banished them.

In private, Jane and I spoke about moving—who would not?—and maybe renting a different house, trying to give full voice to the financial and psychological reasons. Yet try as we might, we mostly talked around it. It was very difficult and painful not only to speak about what had happened, but to admit having been blown so far off our familiar courses in life. What is more, our responses to this murder-suicide had revealed some aspects of our individual natures that were surprisingly different—not opposed to each other, exactly, but quite different. In every vital sense, we were on the same page. But I suspect, too, we were loath to credit that sordid and pernicious act as necessitating anything but a kind of perfect togetherness in order for us to endure. In the end this too would pass; still, since July 16, 2003, each day had required that we fend off estrangements from familiar life, even if they couldn't all be named.

While we convinced each other that doing the radio broadcast with Susan Stamberg would, among other things, exhibit to our friends that we were doing okay, we in fact both had deeply rooted reservations, but mutual encouragement was more important. No regrets there at all, none. However, when I listened to the complete interview, I heard the contrast between Jane's pointillistic honesty and my own impressionistic responses. I recognized Jane's use of an intimate house/body metaphor and my own reliance on ancient parable and literary quotation to articulate what I myself could not. During that interview and in life in general, I was so afraid of self-inflicted despondency that I would outsource all useful insight to others, rather than claim ownership of any original thinking, of how to feel things deeply and say things clearly enough for myself. I started to feel beaten down; all of my reasoning and emotions were generic. However, I did know one thing: out of some misguided attempt to remain stoical, I was making myself physically sick, habituated as I had become to keeping so much sadness inside, along with the seething anger toward Reetika Vazirani. Better that I should have stood on the coast of Nova Scotia and screamed.

On the far more healthy end of the spectrum, Jane, a woman whose house was so violated, was able to dignify her own feelings and pay forthright attention to her concern that all this pain might have lasting effects on our trust and love for each other, and for life itself, and even destroy parts of our very souls. And come to think of it, that first time I listened alone to the radio interview, I tried to gain some knowledge from it, to see if we ourselves were okay. And I thought, Well, yes and no.

As for the "wisdom of the ages" stuff, my therapist said, "For all the lovely altruism of that proverb of David Mamet's you keep referring to — 'If you are walking down the road and see a house on fire . . .'—all well and good, Mr. Norman. But in fact it *was* your house that was violated. You aren't victims, nor are you suggesting anything of the sort, but it *was* your house. If you want to rely on a platitude, why not try 'No good deed goes unpunished,' and see what connection to the truth that provides."

An unforgivable thing had happened. And though we were still in an emotional limbo, life moved on and life moved on. We had book parties, Emma's sleepovers, dinner parties. We had a number of literary-work sojourns apart, Jane and I, and saving-grace periods of time in Vermont. A slow, slow return to normal life.

The thing was, since our house—our actual address—had been made so public, a lot of people we had never met knew where to send mail. In the old life, when any letter arrived, I would open it right away, but after the murder-suicide, I came to dread the mail. If a letter had an unfamiliar postmark or return address, I'd hesitate, sometimes for days, even weeks. One night, looking in a desultory way at a bunch of letters in a basket on my desk, I simply tossed them all out unopened.

Our house was inundated with letters, telephone calls, and e-mails, and some people posted online treatises about what had, or what they thought had, happened there. I could only imagine the types of dialogues about the murder-suicide that went on throughout the literary community. This was human nature, I suppose, the human condition. Speculation, hearsay, eulogies, recriminations. I tried to look at all this as a kind of choral arrangement, a tremendous singing out of innumerable and very conflicted condolences. After all, the phenomenon of poet-suicide, historically speaking, has always been a magnet for all manner of inquiry and debate and hagiography. This public outpouring of emotion was perhaps an attempt to compose the fullest, if inevitably fragmented, presentation of Reetika Vazirani's life and put it to rest. Still, I feel obligated to express my dumbfoundedness that Jehan was so seldom mentioned. The novelist Percival Everett said, straight from the heart, "Why couldn't she have at least let her son live? I am still angry because there were so many ways not to hurt the child. I am sick with the knowledge that his sweet life is over."

Many of these communiqués contained what often felt like a violating sort of presumptuousness, as if there were some shared conviction that my family somehow needed or wanted to collate other people's lettered, and unlettered, opinions into meaningful comprehension of the childhood, upbringing, failed relationships, ambitions, and secrets of this near-total stranger Reetika Vazirani, and as if we had a kinship fascination with the connection—always dubious—between art and madness. (One Washington-area writer, who had claimed to be an intimate of Reetika Vazarani, but in fact had not even known her address, said to me in a bookstore, "A lot of my friends consider me a kind of lay therapist, in case you're interested.")

However, I would also say, even given the sporadic and modest attention I paid to such things, that on the whole these communiqués shared a popular sentiment that Reetika Vazirani's cultural bifurcation (her primary family left Pujab in 1968, when she was six) had somehow mutated into a full-blown bipolar illness. Concerning the so-called (in her own journal) "immigrant condition"—a transitory heart—Reetika Vazirani's sister, Deepika, thought that in her writings her sister "magnified her experience. Maybe she needed a compelling, even fashionable subject. Whatever the reason, Otherness became an enduring theme." And a lot of people theorized that Reetika Vazirani was somehow fatally trapped between viciously contending elements: there was sheer ambition ("Create a buzz around yourself—that's what I did"), there were money worries intensifying the difficulties of single motherhood, and there was antecedent madness (her father had committed suicide). Add to all that her despair about her relationship with Jehan's father, a distinguished poet who lived apart from her and her son.

Perhaps most predictably, literary ambulance chasers—not prone to studied considerations that should better take years—had all sorts of insights about Reetika Vazirani's lines and stanzas. Some of these people suggested that what would come to light was that her writing all along had exhibited, as one correspondent put it, a "posthumous aspect," as if it contained predated keenings from the afterlife. But no poetry is written posthumously; it is only published so, and to suggest that she had clairvoyant powers is as mindless as saying, mistakenly, *suicide-murder.* No, Reetika Vazirani haunted her own writing in real time; she was no ghost at the typewriter, but held pen in living hand.

A number of crazies came out of the woodwork. For example, there was the woman who, in a telephone call, claimed she was representing the British Sylvia Plath Society and wanted to "drop by for a little chat." In another phone call, the leader of a Hindu prayer circle inquired about the possibility of holding its monthly meeting in our house. A doctoral candidate at a college in New York—again on the telephone—said that her thesis was on "creativity and suicide," and asked if she could take photographs of our dining room and, in addition, might we provide photographs "from, you know, *before.* Just so I can have a mode of comparison."

A minor performance artist from Southern California sent an invitation to attend a performance of *Medea* in which she somehow played all the parts. And then there was the time I picked up the telephone and heard a woman say, "Hello, I'm a teacher and scholar from Pakistan. And I'm writing about what V. S. Naipaul called 'forensic memoir.' I immediately hung up. What could she possibly have wanted? A letter arrived asking us to vacate our house for an evening so that a group that held séances "specializing in artists" could carry out its mandate. The producer of a television show about paranormal activity found me having a cup of coffee in the café at Politics & Prose bookstore, and immediately wanted to set up a camera and lighting crew in the dining room of my house: "We're the least invasive of any of the programs in our field."

More and more and more. To the point where I wondered, My goodness, what sort of world do we live in? And really, what did I know for sure? What did I really know? Perhaps only that this thing had been *visited upon us,* that my deepest sympathies lay with my wife and daughter, that next in my hierarchy of sympathies were friends and family who felt deeply for us. And I knew that violence of this nature had occurred through the millennia, in countless houses, in countless cities and villages, and unfortunately in our house, too. I also knew that no single fact could possibly provide any—my most despised word—*closure.* However, I hoped that the passage of time might allow for perspective.

A year went by.

I did not allow myself to expect life to contain, for quite some time to come, as much joy as I had previously felt. I believed that to expect otherwise would almost require a new category of optimism. The scaffolding, the framework, for joy had been rebuilt; it was rickety; I hadn't dared to climb up on it yet. When I use the word *joy* here, I mean a reliable, compelling—and, yes, at times even transcendent—duet between a melancholy natural to my character and irony. It's just my own definition, of course. So that when I sat up late into the night and thought about it, I realized that over the previous year, in the main when joy arrived, it was more a simulacrum. Almost but not quite recognizable as joy. I thought, Well, at least I comprehend the problem, the frustration, the longing to change this condition. As early as age nineteen, on my first visit to Point Reyes National Seashore, I discovered that watching shore birds was a trusted way of transforming a simulacrum of joy into, at least by my lights, authentic joy. And now I wanted joy back, pure and simple, because if you don't have it, you start to experience what Keats called "a posthumous existence." And I was terribly afraid of this.

One of my favorite writers, Ryunosuke Akutagawa, asked, "What good is intelligence if you cannot discover a useful melancholy?" I've found that melancholy can often be an intensifying element in humor, and conversely, humor can, as Akutagawa suggests, make melancholy more useful in refining a philosophy of life.

And so in early July of 2004 I traveled to California to look at shore birds. Jane stayed in Vermont, still shell-shocked but writing poems again—living her life. Emma was taking a zillion photographs, and she would soon have friends staying in the farmhouse while they rehearsed *Hamlette* (a female-centered and outlandishly comic version of *Hamlet*), to be performed in Craftsbury Common, Vermont, where, all summer, a new steeple and steeple bell were being installed in the Methodist church.

From the San Francisco airport, I drove a rental car north on Route 1, past Muir Woods, stopped for lunch at Stinson Beach, and continued on to Olema. I checked into the Olema Inn and by two o'clock was at McClures Beach near Pierce Point Historic Ranch, all of which is part of the Point Reyes National Seashore.

Throughout that first afternoon at McClures Beach, the heat was counterbalanced by sea breezes, whitecaps glinted in the sun, and the sea alternated between blue-grey and blue, depending on how the light presented it. In small flocks and individual presences, flying in, flying off, skittering along the beach, I saw sandpipers, dowitchers, surfbirds, willets, tattlers, turnstones, and plovers. At times they made for a riotous neighborhood of birds, and then, as if a crosswind had erased all life, the beach was suddenly bereft of them. I loved, as I have always loved, watching sanderlings hustle about and forage with their bills as if trying to stitch in place the wavering margin between tide and beach, a margin that soaks away with every wave. (I wondered once if this was the inspiration for invisible ink.) And high aloft over the cliffs, hawks and vultures were kiting the thermals. Late one afternoon I saw an enormous charcoal-hued, zeppelin-shaped cloud drop a curtain of rain, which was spectrally backlit by a glow from the farther sea. And soon a flock of pelicans flew straight out of that rain, as if it were an ancient form of bathing. The pelicans arrived and congregated on the beach, bellying out individual hammocks of sand, muttering, bickering, bill-clacking, and then all at once shut down all utterances, tucking into themselves for a communal nap.

I spent the next couple of hours mucking about the tide pools, taking in the sun, not doing much at all, trying not to think, and then in the light of early dusk a western oystercatcher landed on a small rock island and emitted its characteristic piping whistle, *kee-ap kee-ap wee-o.* This bird is dusty black and has pale legs, a bright orange bill, and a rim of orange-red around its eyes. I watched this oystercatcher probe every nook and cranny, concentrate every use of its bill, poking, jabbing, laboring to pry up the most tenaciously adhesive of mollusks.

Slowly the exhaustion of travel and the drowsiness from sun and sea air accumulated and I almost fell asleep standing up. Noting the condition of the tide, I walked back from the water thirty or so yards, lay down on the sand, and dozed off, only to be awoken in late dusk by the riotous noise of at least fifty seagulls. There were three different species of gulls, all drawn to a dead dolphin. The dolphin, now dull-skinned and splotched with sand, must have tumbled in while I was asleep.

At their rapacious scavenging, the gulls were surprisingly unfazed by a rather tall woman dressed in a dark green rain slicker, blue jeans, and laceless hiking boots, her dark blond hair tied at the top of her head in a dreadlocked mop, standing not more than five feet away from the dolphin. She was working a tripod camera. Now and then as I watched through binoculars, I saw a gull feign a skirmish with the photographer, hovering in midair, cough-shrieking like a rusty well pump, yet the woman went on adjusting her lens, taking photographs of the dolphin's carcass, jotting something in her notebook tied by a string to her belt.

I watched this until most of the daylight was out over the sea and the cliffs threw shadows on the beach, and then I set out for the trail back up to the gravel parking lot. At the top of the rise, when I turned to look back, there was just enough light to see that many gulls were taloned to the dolphin, wildly flapping their wings as if trying to carry it away to a secret lair for the night. Their squalls and cries echoed up the beach as the photographer packed up her equipment and lit a cigarette.

I drove back to the Olema Inn, seeing a bobcat scatter across the road into the tall, dry grass and weeds, and hawks perched on fence posts as the night came on fully. I had a mango salad at the inn's restaurant, then sat in jeans, T-shirt, light sweater, and loafers on the side porch, drinking a glass of wine, watching swallows and the occasional bat zigzag and careen after insects. In the cooling night air the fragrance of a nearby stand of eucalyptus was deeply—and familiarly—stirring, and I felt gratified that the day had gone as it had. Then, at around eight-thirty, a rattle-trap 1960s Volvo, with two hubcaps missing and a faulty muffler, pulled into the parking area, and when its driver crouched out I saw that it was the photographer. She carried her tripod camera and a leather satchel, her boots slung around her neck, and she was barefoot. When she stepped up to the porch I said, "You were with that dolphin, weren't you?"

"Oh, that was you," she said. "Yeah, I noticed somebody up the beach. I was annoyed. I prefer to be out there alone. I'm usually out there alone."

"Join the club."

She reached out her hand for me to shake and said, "I'm Halley, last name's spelled S-h-a-g-r-a-n—pronounced *chagrin*."

I laughed and introduced myself. "Does your last name explain why you're drawn to sad sights like that dolphin?"

"Wow, that's pretty funny," she said. "And pretty personal. But you know what? That dolphin was definitely not a sad sight for me."

"How so?"

"Because death happens in nature and I like to take pictures of it. The way I look at it, the beaches are always full of such news — natural-history news, I call it. The dolphin was like an obituary from the sea. There's hundreds a day."

"Interesting how you put things."

"Interesting or not, that's my thinking. Know what else? I don't mind calling myself a nature photographer. I don't mind if somebody buys a photograph of mine because they enjoy nature. That's cool. Life for me has a spiritual affirmation and so does death. That was quite an earful, huh?"

"I'd like to see some of your work."

"I only use black-and-white film. And you know what—and I can't verify this—I only dream in black and white, I'm pretty sure. My husband, Sonam, says that in a past life I was colorblind. He tends to say stuff like that. He's a Buddhist. I mean a Tibetan Buddhist. I mean a born-and-raised-in-Tibet Buddhist."

"Did you meet in Tibet?"

Halley sat on the bench beside me; an acrid whiff of what had to be the dolphin snapped in my nostrils, and when Halley noticed me noticing this, she said, "Yeah, well, I was just going up for a bath. But to answer your question, no, we didn't meet in Tibet. But we got married there. No, I'd been teaching an introduction to photography class on the UC Berkeley campus. Sonam was late for a lecture he was giving in physiology, he'd got lost trying to find the lecture room, and he wandered in. I was in the darkroom, and one of my students sent him in to get directions from me, but I didn't know where his lecture room was either. He had the wrong part of campus, I told him that much. But that's how we first met. After that he came to the darkroom, like, twenty days in a row or something."

"Thanks for telling me. It's a good story."

"Sonam and I live in Mendocino, but I'm photographing here at Point Reyes so often, it's sort of a home away from home. My husband has a medical practice that keeps him very busy."

"What kind of medicine does he practice?"

"Regular old general practitioner, though I guess that's kinda rare these days, huh? He went to medical school in London. A lot of people hear that my husband's Tibetan and right away they figure he's into some kind of freaky-deaky medicine. And sure, he tells patients to try alternative medicines of all sorts if they want. Of course he does. And he's even studying serious acupuncture. But he always wanted just to put out a shingle like in a Norman Rockwell painting, you know? Except our little family joke is, Norman Rockwell never painted Tibetans."

"What does Sonam think of your photographs? That's personal, I know."

"Why not ask him yourself? You could have dinner with us."

"That's nice of you, but the restaurant here's a bit pricey."

"How about that little white clapboard place near the turnoff to Inverness?"

"Pretty late for dinner, isn't it, or not?"

"How's nine o'clock—they serve till nine-thirty. Come on. Sonam will be pleased. He says I'm an antisocial hermit. *Hermitess*."

With obviously long-practiced dispatch, Halley unraveled her dreadlocks into a waterfall of hair and said, "I'm surprised a seagull didn't fall out."

I went up to my room to put on a pair of socks and grab a jacket. My notebook was open to that favorite Robert Frost line from "A Servant to Servants," "the best way out is always through," which had become a kind of talisman along the journey from Mathilde in 1969 to the murder-suicide to this moment in room 1 of the Olema Inn.

When I sat down to dinner with Halley and Sonam, every table in the restaurant was occupied. The menu was in French and English, and our waitress alerted us to her limited patience after a long night of waiting tables. "If any of you are in the mood to practice your French," she said, "I'm not." Sonam ordered in French and so did Halley, but I did not have the language. Our table was on the slatwood veranda near a eucalyptus tree.

Sonam was fifteen years older than Halley and at least five inches shorter. He was neatly dressed in grey jeans, starched white shirt, penny loafers. He had a handsome face and short-cropped black hair and sported round tortoiseshell glasses. "Halley thinks I look like Mr. Moto in these specs," he said. We chatted about this and that. Sonam asked what sort of books I wrote, and when our food arrived Halley said, "Sonam, our new friend here asked me what you thought of my photographs."

Frowning in an exaggerated way, Sonam said, "Well, do you mean my opinion of her technical skill, the aesthetic quality of her pictures? Or what it's like to have a house full of—let's see: seagulls torn to shreds, festering whale carcasses, seals with hollowed-out eye sockets, ummm, what else? Oh, yes, there's an eviscerated bobcat, vultures poking their heads inside a mule deer—and Halley told me you saw her hanging around a dolphin today."

I set down my fork and stared at my food as if I'd lost my appetite. "Maybe I shouldn't have asked the question," I said, and there was laughter all around.

"Actually, Halley sees herself as a . . . Darling, how do you say it? A chronicler of transitional states."

"Meaning," I said, "you think the dolphin was on its way to being reincarnated."

"Yep, *transitional* could mean that," Halley said. "But it could also mean just turning into organic stuff, you know? Food for beetles. Seagulls turning it to shit that drops on your windshield. It's all pretty straightforward, don't you think?"

"As for the artistic part," Sonam said, "I'm her greatest admirer."

"By the way, what were you doing out there today?" Halley asked me. "Are you a *birder*? God help us. Probably not the sort I hate, because you had those cheapo field glasses."

"No, not that sort of birder, if I understand you correctly. Though I'd love a better pair of binoculars, that's for sure."

I suppose I could have delicately alluded, in a way that might have honestly addressed Halley's question but at the same time indicated my discomfort in dwelling on the subject, to the haunting incident that had occurred in my house. In turn I could have said that I'd come out to Point Reyes to lose myself among shore birds, to walk every trail until I could hardly walk another step, to empty out physically and mentally, then get filled again. But for goodness' sake, if the best way out is always through, it didn't mean one couldn't afford to take a moment away from the effort. Besides, I thought that to foist all of that bleakness on these kind, engaging folks at our candlelit table, with a full moon rising, during such a get-to-know-each-other meal, would be, as we used to say in the sixties, too heavy.

But I'd had a little too much wine and said, "Out at McClures Beach I wanted to be invisible for a few hours, go out there on the rocks, all that sun and big waves, and sit right next to an oyster-catcher, and it would look up every so often, sensing something was there, but then go about being an oystercatcher again." And I don't know what got into me, but I added, "Amen."

My existential riff had the effect that is sometimes the case when something of staggering pretentiousness or insufferable sentimentality, however genuine, is spoken: it caused an eyes-cast-to-table silence for a moment. Then Sonam ordered espresso for himself and Halley.

"You know," Halley said, "I might have two or three photographs of oystercatchers. Sonam, would you mind looking in my studio when you get home tomorrow? You know, the photographs are filed away in alphabetical order. If you find oystercatchers, bring them back Friday so our friend here can have a look."

After dinner I sat again on the porch of the inn; the late-night air drew out the fragrance of eucalyptus even more intensely. I thought of Nabokov's phrase "memory perfume." The inn's resident, almost lynx-sized cat, Truffle, bounded up onto my lap, a very well-fed animal, and settled in nicely. She allowed me to comb her back with my fingers, and whenever I made the effort to lift and set her down, she dug in with her claws. I quickly understood that this cat would decide when she was through with me.

Mulling it over, I was not so sure I wanted to see photographs of dead oystercatchers just when I was becoming so engaged with the lively oystercatcher I'd seen at McClures Beach and hoped to see much of during the next ten days. Perhaps Sonam wouldn't find the photographs. I hoped he wouldn't.

But sitting in the eucalyptus breeze, feeling Truffle's growl-purr roll in a kind of gentle, seismic wave from head to tail, with nothing to do but wait for the familiar, advanced signs of insomnia, I thought hard and with some uneasiness about why I had been so willing to subscribe to Halley's reductionist philosophy of life and death. Why couldn't I muster up a response that was more natural to my character, something caustic, or at least probing? Why didn't I confirm, if only in my private thoughts, that death in fact is not "all pretty straightforward"? Of course we'd really just met, but that was not it. Maybe Halley's platitudes offered solace, in the way a beautiful landscape can offer solace. If you are fortunate and willing, you can live inside it with perfect equanimity.

At dinner I'd been impressed by Halley's phrase "eddies of wet feathers" to describe what she was reminded of when she looked at her photograph of a dead crow she'd recently developed in a darkroom in Point Reyes Station. When I went up to my room at about two a.m., that photograph was leaning against my door. Taped to it was a note:

See the moon? It's about 1:30 a.m. now and in an hour I'm heading out to McClures Beach. Sonam may or may not go with me. Nobody's supposed to be out there at night but you can only see certain things at night. So that's where I'll be — since you seem interested in my work. By the way, oystercatchers sometimes are active at night, if there's a big moon and so on, little known fact. But I've seen that. Halley.

Generous invitation, I thought, and sat down on the overstuffed chair in my room, switched on the floor lamp, and looked at the photograph. I saw the eddies: three stilled whorls of black feathers on the crow's mangled body, and each appeared to be sculpted by a waterspout. Studying the picture, I went from being almost repelled by the eerie vortexes to imagining what a mercy it must have been for the bird to blink out of consciousness, to perish, all evidence indicating ("Almost every bone was broken," Halley had said) that the crow had been tumultuously storm-tossed, spun, and sent crashing to the ground. In other words, I was beginning to see things from Halley's point of view, and in that I found a reprieve, because I was sick and tired of my own morbid distress about life and death and what felt like my painful dislocation of soul.

I set aside the photograph, took up my paperback copy of Frost's poems, and read through "A Servant to Servants" (whose narrator admits that she has been away in the state asylum), and while reading heard mourning doves, which I'd never heard before at night. Just in the past five minutes my new education in birds — Halley's experience of seeing oystercatchers, and my hearing the doves — made for interesting speculations about the role of moonlight in extending the diurnal activities of birds on into the nighttime hours. I fell asleep in my clothes, crosswise on the bed.

Now, I'm more than aware that relating a dream makes most people's eyes glaze over as they morph into the figure on the bridge in Edvard Munch's *The Scream*. But the dream of mine I want to tell illustrates Rilke's idea that the unspeakable is quite capable of intervening on any normal day of waking, breathing in the hours, and dreaming. Anyway, my dream was set in a Chinese restaurant in the North Beach section of San Francisco; I recognized the location because, looking out the window, I saw City Lights bookstore. Sonam, Halley, and I had just completed a feast; bowls, plates, chopsticks, glasses, and teacups were on the table. Sonam and Halley read their fortunes and shared them with each other; Halley looked at me and said, "Same old, same old." Out of nowhere, an ancient-looking hag with beautiful cat's eyes — I think they were Truffle's — threw herself onto our table. Shocked, frightened, Halley and Sonam pushed their chairs back. The old woman clamped my face between her hands (their texture was like sandpaper) and shouted, "*I beg you, don't read your fortunes! Don't read your fortunes!*" I was aware of being puzzled about why she used the plural *fortunes*, since there was only a single fortune cookie remaining in the porcelain bowl. Then, in a phantasmagoric locution, a squalling flock of seagulls flew in, lit on the hag's shoulders, lifted and carried her off, out the door and in the direction of the ocean.

The restaurant, absent waiters, cooks, and other customers, was now fog-ridden and cold. For some reason I snapped open my fortune cookie. A bunch of fortunes sprang out, as if in a heart-attack surprise from a jack-in-the-box, and rose to the ceiling, where each was caught by the tongue of a magnificently painted dragon. A wooden ladder with wheels presented itself, and I climbed it to the top rung and read the fortunes, going from dragon mouth to dragon mouth. As it turned out, they were not the sardonic witticisms or prefabricated proverbs we generally associate with fortune cookies. Instead they were—and I comprehended it right then and there in the dream—replications of entries in those three-by-five black notebooks Reetika Vazirani had tried to hide, or hide in plain sight.

I startled awake in my bed at the Olema Inn, sweating, with a terrible headache, the knowledge of what those fortune cookies contained having crossed over into consciousness. The alarm clock on the bedside table read 3:50 a.m.; I could hear the voice of an owl, but that lovely sound did not prevent me from feeling disoriented, near to the point of weeping. My thoughts were frazzled, and I said to myself, "Look, you can't help where your mind goes in sleep."

The telephone on the table rang: it was the front desk, the night clerk reporting that my next-door neighbors in room 2 had lodged a complaint about "loud talk—even screaming." I apologized but did not say that I had had a nightmare. I thought the best thing would be to drive to McClures Beach to see what Halley Shagran might be up to. Extend the night that was so rudely interrupted, take in the air, the moonlight.

Halfway into my drive to Pierce Point Historic Ranch, I experienced a reprise of the all too familiar, cramped tightening of gloom in my stomach, a minor attack of nausea, the sense of a threaded pulse, so I immediately pulled into a turnoff along the road. I got out and leaned against the car, taking as many deep breaths as I could. What was this? What was happening? The moon was so beautiful over the ocean. There was a strong wind off the sea, a shushing whisper of it in the conifers close by to my right, and far off in the distance to my left, the constellation of lights and the vague outline of a behemoth freighter slowly moving north.

Despite my headache and nausea, I got back in the car and drove slowly, and when I got to Pierce Point and parked in the lot, I took a high-intensity flashlight, got out of the car, and followed the long, wide beam down the path to McClures Beach. Moonlight flooded the beach, but there was no sign of Halley, and I hadn't seen her car anywhere in the vicinity of Pierce Point, either. I walked down the beach toward the cliffs. Sprawling, tentacled bulbs of medusa kelp lay here and there—you can easily slip on them. I walked past the dolphin carcass, which, on quick inspection by flashlight, had been considerably picked apart, but there was still enough left for the carrion gulls at first light.

I continued on to the stretch of beach between the cliffs and the archipelago of small rock islands where I'd seen the oystercatcher. Feeling on my skin the cold balm of fog, I ventured out onto a peninsula of coral-jagged rock and stood there, hoping the sea breeze would move straight through my head, ear to ear, taking those horrid fortunes with it. And that is when I heard the oystercatcher.

Was it the same one? I thought it must be, since oystercatchers are solitary and territorial birds. While at first I couldn't locate the oystercatcher in the gauzy, spectral light, I kept hearing its plaintive *kee-ap kee-ap wee-o*. And after ten minutes or so I saw the bird itself, and seeing it, I recognized the ventriloquial talent of the beach at night — the oystercatcher sounded as if it were farther north than it actually was. I moved twenty yards up from the peninsula and huddled in a rain slicker and blanket on dry sand beneath the cliffs, where I stayed the rest of the night, the oystercatcher appearing and disappearing until the mist burned off and the daytime world, with its ocean light, was revealed. Pelicans flew in formation low to the water, and seals bobbed offshore in the background — with the dead dolphin in the foreground, in repose, as yet free of scavenging gulls.

Roughly an hour after dawn broke, the oystercatcher flew off but was back within the hour. Where had it gone? The bird began to work its rock island again. I watched its frantic industriousness, its fluttering up a foot or two and back down to the rocks, its preening, and then Halley showed up with her camera and notebook.

Postcards, telephone calls, and the poems of Robert Frost kept me connected to Vermont, but by and large I felt like a resident, for those ten days, of Point Reyes National Seashore. I had taken to wearing a T-shirt with my favorite painting on it, Milton Avery's *California Landscape/Seascape,* depicting a house and several outbuildings above a steep-cliffed horseshoe-shaped inlet, surrounded by fields of tawny brown and yellow dry grasses. And during the next eight days — and all through two nights — I accompanied Halley Shagran on her photographic traipses along beaches and trails, through wetland and woodland, all of which were, after my many visits to this preserve, as familiar as the palm of my hand. Yet as she narrated her own past experiences, railed against local anti-conservationists, imparted all sorts of zoological and botanical information, I came to see these old places in a new light. "Let's face it," she said, "I make photographic autopsies and never run out of subject matter." I even became affectionately accustomed to her offbeat humor.

Simply put, I felt that by being so artistically absorbed in death's spell, Halley had come to cast her own spell on death. I watched her photograph gulls, pelicans, weasels, seals, sea lions, foxes, kestrels, mule deer, axis deer, butterflies, beetles, and cattle, each animal discovered in its final posture, in a stage of decomposition, with its fixed stare, its agonized or oddly peaceful expression, its corporeal disarray. All of which would eventually be depicted in black and white, like negatives of creation itself, in the photographs Halley developed late into most nights in the darkroom at Point Reyes Station.

I estimated that, apart from my time with Halley, I watched my oystercatcher for roughly fifty hours on that visit. The oystercatcher's existence offered me a hypnotic passage of time, a vicarious connection to the sea, and focus, distraction, sorrow, laughter, tears, all helping to move me *through* and escape the grasp of servitude to the fixed notion that only pain and sorrow are real truths, and that joy exists only to be subject to doubt. That is, at least in some provisional way, after all those hours in the realm of the oystercatcher, I was feeling joy as opposed to a simulacrum of joy, a condition that just might warrant use of the word *healing*. On my last afternoon at McClures Beach, I thought, When the spirit of this wonderful oystercatcher *transitions*, I hope it becomes an oystercatcher.

As I write this, in a house in Inverness, California, in the early-morning hours, with deer nibbling apples fallen from a craggy tree, a flock of pelicans in view high over Tomales Bay, a stack of letters on the dining room table, a manual typewriter there, too, after having had a breakfast of orange juice, cranberry scones, and coffee, I'm reading the posthumously published collection of poems, *Radha Says*, written by Reetika Vazirani. I notice that many of the poems have, as part of their narrative strategy, a broken-line form, caesuras imposing what Igor Stravinsky called "the exigencies of an interval." In part what he meant was that silence between musical notes contains as much complexity, as much earned and rendered feeling, as the notes themselves. You could argue that the same idea applies to a Morse code message delivering alarming news.

Now, I am far from being a poet. But I subscribe to what W. H. Auden thought, that truly original poetry is the purest air language can breathe, and to sully that air by overdramatizing the abject soul makes fraudulent claims on the reader's heart. And I subscribe to what Zadie Smith wrote: "No geographic or racial qualification guarantees a writer her subject . . . Only interest, knowledge, and love will do that." And I am recalling what Alfred de Vigny wrote: "A calm despair . . . is the essence of wisdom."

With these devoted beliefs and assertions, like vigilant sentinels posted near at hand—as if these writers were standing just yards away on the wooden veranda of this house—I struggle and reread, struggle and reread. Finally I detect faint suggestions of joy in many of the persona poems, with their voices of the Urdu poet Ghalib and the Radha of Hindu epic—but also find much theosophical confusion and misanthropy. I suppose that I experience this whole collection as a libretto for the staging of a solipsistic and garish mytho-opera, with each poem an evocation of real suffering. But more concretely, while reading I keep picturing a woman in India—perhaps a poet, perhaps not. She stands in a house, on a woven rug, an heirloom trod upon by children and adults—possibly representing the sheer fabric of daily life—that is worn threadbare, definitely unraveling.

My sentinels on the veranda are shooed away—be gone!— and sitting at the round, glass-topped table, in bare feet in the sun now, I am daydreaming the peacefulness of my farmhouse in Vermont, its gently curving road up to my neighbors' mailboxes, mountains visible in the distance. I think of the wetlands near Port Medway, Nova Scotia, with thunderstorms and fishing trawlers on the horizon. What to look forward to today? Well, for one thing, I will not leave this house. Let the world arrive as it may; I will read all of *The Apple Trees at Olema,* by Robert Hass, who lives just up the road, a lifetime of poems containing such indispensable human sadness and joy, and which are as sanely associative as the finest of Cezanne's paintings, and strike the deepest chords. There is a cleansing light over Tomales Bay after a nightlong rain. The death of a boy named Jehan nearly ten years ago was not the fault of poetry. I close my eyes. There's the oystercatcher, arriving at the same archipelago of rocks as always. It flies off, it returns. It flies off, and after a long time, during which I worry over its fate, it returns.